The ***Failure Free*** Reading Methodology

New Hope for Non-Readers

By
Dr. Joseph **Lockavitch**

First published by Dog Ear Publishing
4010 W. 86th Street, Ste H
Indianapolis, IN 46268
www.dogearpublishing.net

ISBN: 978-159858-305-2

This book is printed on acid-free paper.

Printed in the United States of America

Table of Contents

Forward

Here are three indisputable reading facts. Nobody can deny them. These facts have stood the test of time.

1. Students are failing to read.
2. Students will continue to fail to read.
3. One of these students might be yours.

Reading failure in our schools and our society is a major issue. There are over 24 million functional illiterates in the United States. Every year, over 800,000 students drop out of school.

The prisons are at capacity—most with prisoners who cannot read above a third grade level. Businesses are investing billions of dollars in programs to upgrade the literacy skills of their own employees.

Fortunately, given all of this, there is one fact that is more important: reading failure can be treated and prevented.

One of the biggest problems facing parents and teachers today has been the need for a fast acting, easy to use literacy program for non-readers: students and adults who have an independent reading level between 0.0 and 3.0. This deep need is something of which I have first hand knowledge.

During the past 30 years, as a former classroom teacher, special education director, school psychologist, and university professor, I have been involved in the plight of the non-reader. My initial involvement began shortly after I had finished a training session with a group of teachers for learning disabled students. I had just finished a session summarizing the most commonly used remedial reading approaches. When I finished, the participants echoed a theme I had heard many times before, "We appreciate what you have told us and the approaches you mentioned look very good—especially for those students with mild to moderate reading needs," they said, "but what about the kids who can't read a lick?" one teacher asked, "What are we to do all day with these non-readers?"

A Nagging Question

The question of what to do with non-readers was one that had also bothered me when I was a special education teacher. I noticed, first hand, a huge difference between the terms "struggling readers" and "non-readers." While all of the remedial programs had value for "struggling readers" (students as many as four years behind), they simply did not work for a hard-core group of non-readers. I was still meeting students who continually defied conventional instruction. I tried everything I knew and yet, they were still failing miserably; I could not reach them. No matter how hard I tried (and boy, did I try) they still were no better off. And so, I asked myself, "What could be done? What could be done to impact on the lives of these students who are dying on the literacy vine?" Little did I know that I was about to embark on a thirty-year journey.

Thirty years of trying to find a solution to one ongoing problem. Thirty years of trying to rescue the lives of millions of students who are drowning in the classroom. Should I stop? No, I cannot stop when these students actually are growing in numbers. Even worse, the system is creating them every day thanks to the constant arguing, backbiting and a "one size fits all" mentality.

Stop the Either/Or Approach

I began to look at the two basic approaches to the teaching of reading. These two approaches are still dominant today. The more I studied the position taken by the proponents of each philosophy, the more I was reminded of an old TV commercial. The commercial centered on defining the product—what the product really was. Was it a breath mint or a candy mint? The commercial involved two people defending the opposite point of view. One person would scream "It's a breath mint!" while the other person would scream back "No, you're wrong, it's a candy mint!" Both people were absolutely sure they were right and that the other person was wrong. They were at what appeared to be an unsolvable impasse. Finally, at the end of the commercial, an unseen announcer would state: "Stop, you're both right! They're two, two mints in one!" It seems the same holds true today in the teaching of reading, both philosophies are right! Unfortunately, when it comes to the plight of the non-reader, both philosophies are wrong—dead wrong!

Reading is not an either/or approach for our non-readers. Reading is not either phonics or whole language. Reading is much more complicated than that. Reading is an interactive process that involves giving non-readers (regardless of age) simultaneous access to the three instructional elements crucial to reading success. In other words, non-readers, regardless of age, must be in highly repetitive materials, written in a basic sentence structure and containing content that is easy to relate to. Sadly, none of the existing reading approaches utilize materials that control for simultaneous access to these critical elements. So, armed with this knowledge I set out to create a reading methodology that did.

Chapter One

What Are the Assumed Causes
of Reading Failure?

Traditional Beliefs

There are many popular theories about why students fail to read. Generally, these factors are either internal (found within the student) or external (contained within the approach). The most common internal factors mentioned are:

1. Lack of Motivation
2. Perceptual Disorders
3. Intellectual Deficits
4. Lack of Readiness

Let us go a little more in depth and discuss each one of these theories.

Lack of Motivation

"I try the best I can. I vary my approaches. I'm enthusiastic. I try my best to make learning a fun and enjoyable experience. Yet, nothing seems to work. My students don't respond. They do not try. It's as if they could care less."

To many teachers, the preceding statements are not uncommon. Nothing is more frustrating than trying your best and getting nothing for it. When this happens, is there any wonder why teachers see lack of motivation as a primary cause of reading difficulties?

Not only are teachers all too familiar with the previous scenario but many parents can also relate to this great anxiety. What are they to do when they hear from school that their child is not motivated? How are they supposed to respond? What can they do to help motivate their child?

Often, students are being accused of not caring, when in fact, they are giving it all they can. If we only knew the pain in their heart or the shame they feel or the years and years of frustration that they have experienced.

So, is lack of motivation the real culprit?

Blaming Reading Failure on Motivation

There are many problems associated with blaming reading failure on motivation. Our ability to measure motivation is the biggest problem we face. Motivation cannot be measured anymore than we can give precise measurements to the amount of love or hate someone has within them. Motivation cannot be measured because it cannot be observed. It is not concrete. It is an abstract concept. Motivation is inferred. It is something attributed to someone by someone else.

Confused? Don't be. Consider the following example. Teachers might attribute lack of motivation to the following observable classroom behaviors: failure to do assignments, or not answering a question, or a particular facial expression. But are they right? Is this really due to a lack of motivation or could there be another explanation?

I once wrote about a situation where a teacher was sure lack of motivation was the prime reason a boy in her class was failing. The boy was six years old and had been described by this teacher as a child who refused to do his work, even though he knew how to do it. "All he does is just sit there. And I know he knows it," said his teacher.

When I went over to the boy, I saw that he was expected to complete a skills worksheet. The work sheet was designed to teach the initial consonant "h." On the sheet were a series of drawings, most of which began with the "h" sound. The dominant drawing (well over half the page) consisted of a picture of a hippopotamus. Next to this picture was the letter "h" with additional space for the pupil to write an accompanying "h." When I asked the boy if he knew what to do, he replied "yes." Not being fully convinced and knowing that recognizing the picture of a hippopotamus was the key to success, I asked him to tell me about the picture. "Oh sure," he said, "That's a picture of a pig!"

The preceding example illustrates just how subjective the assessment of motivation was. The teacher, who was so sure the boy was failing because of a lack of motivation, had made an incorrect assumption. The boy did not know what was expected of him. Because he saw a pig, rather than a hippo, this particular activity sheet made no sense to him, and because of this, he chose to wait for further instruction.

Teacher Frustration

Why was the teacher so sure it was "lack of motivation"? It was because she did not know otherwise. She knew she had tried her best and she had done everything—straight by the book—and yet, the boy was still failing. She had no other alternatives available to her. From her perspective, the boy's "lack of motivation" was the problem. This was not a vindictive label but her only alternative.

Too often, pronounced reading failure is seen as an either/or situation. The problem lies either with the teacher or with the child. This is not correct. There are other reasons why students fail, even with the best teachers, and in most cases the highest levels of student motivation.

Give Failing Students Credit

Failing students are not given the credit they deserve.

Puzzled? I will say it again. Most students with pronounced reading failure should be applauded for their exceptionally high level of motivation. Let me explain.

Imagine being born fabulously wealthy. All you will ever need and want is yours for the asking. Everyday is a vacation.

Now imagine living in total poverty. Everyday you awake to the sensation of hunger in your stomach. You own nothing. Everyday is survival.

Ask this question: which life requires the greater degree of motivation just to get up in the morning? Most would agree that the second illustration demands the higher degree of motivation.

Live or Die

The second person has only two choices: live or die. Given these circumstances, many might wonder why they would continue to go on. But they do. It is a matter of survival. And as we all know, survival is a great motivator.

The same holds true for our millions of failing students. Every day they wake up to go to school and fail. They must go. They have no choice. The law demands it. Like it or not, they wake up knowing they will fail for the next six hours. They wake up knowing they will fail five days a week. They wake up knowing they will fail for the next thirty-five weeks (not counting summer school). Like it or not, they wake up knowing they will fail for at least the next ten years. They will continue to fail until they are finally old enough to drop out of school and stop the pain.

Think of the guts it must take to walk in their shoes. Think of the pure determination it has to take knowing that they are going to be made fun of or to feel foolish and stupid again and again. However, despite all that, still they go and still they try. No motivation? No way! Not even close!

Lack of Motivation Makes No Sense

The notion that failing students lack motivation makes no sense. Why? Because the consequences of failing grades make such an assumption inconceivable. Who would trade success for failure, acceptance for scorn, or respect for ridicule? No one. Not you or me and especially not these students. No one likes to fail. It is against human nature. In many cases, our failing students are trying too hard and paying too heavy a price as the following two examples illustrate.

Too Heavy a Toll

The first example involved an eight-year-old girl who developed a bleeding ulcer. Her parents blamed most of it on her reaction to reading failure and the classroom punishment she received.

It seems that students who did not perform up to standard in this young girl's class were selected for special attention. Failing students were to sit in a corner under a large stool. The teacher had reserved this corner for students who were not doing what they should.

According to the girl's parents, every day she was asked to read and every day she ended up in that corner under that stool. Imagine going to bed every night knowing you had to go back to that corner and sit under that stool. Yet, she did it. She did it every day for a year, and all she got from it was a bleeding ulcer and poor grades. No motivation? Oh, come on now.

The Boy Who Always Wore a Cap to School

The second example concerns a seven-year-old boy who also wanted to read very badly. I first met him when I was running a summer reading clinic for a major southeastern university. I was intrigued with the boy because for six weeks this boy always came to our clinic with a baseball cap on his head. He never took the cap off. Not for one minute or second within our clinic. Rain or shine, warm or cold, this seven-year-old second grader wore that cap and he refused to take it off. I had to find out why.

I soon discovered the reason. I found out that this boy could have been the poster child for school failure. While only seven years old, this boy was a virtual non-reader who had already been retained once in kindergarten, a second time in first grade and was going to be retained a third time if he failed to show any improvement this summer. Given this knowledge, I made the incorrect assumption that perhaps the reason for the cap was a deep-seated need for security or comfort. Wrong—not even close!

This seven year old was wearing the cap for a more utilitarian reason. The cap served a much-needed purpose. The cap kept a secret. And what was this secret? The secret was the fact that this seven-year-old boy was rapidly going bald! That's right! His hair was actually falling out in patches or clumps. Why was this child going bald? The reason was pure and simple: anxiety.

The boy had a condition known as "alopecia areata," or baldness in localized areas. Although its cause is unknown, severe psychological stress seems to be a primary factor. In other words, this boy was so anxious to read that his hair was falling out. What could be a greater sign of motivation?

One Final Observation

I would like to add one final observation concerning student motivation and reading failure. It concerns what appears to be a natural desire on the part of students to learn to read.

I once worked as a Headstart teacher. Headstart is a federally funded program designed to give lower-income minority preschool students a chance to catch up to their middle-class peers.

What impressed me the most about my students was their universal attraction to books. They were fascinated with the mystery of print. They loved to hear stories read aloud. Moreover, they very much wanted to learn how to read.

What concerned me, however, was the research showing how many of these very motivated preschoolers would eventually be placed in remedial reading programs by the third grade with the primary reason being cited as a lack of motivation. My question? What caused such an abrupt change toward reading on the part of these highly motivated preschoolers? What could have possibly turned off their "highly motivated switch" by the end of third grade?

Perceptual Disorders

The front-page cover story features a photograph of a young girl. Behind her is a chalkboard. One word is on the chalkboard. The word is misspelled. A lowercase "b" replaces the "d." The word is "byslexia."

The poster depicts a school scene. The word "school" is written in a child's handwriting. The "s" in school is backwards. The caption reads: Imagine what school would be like if this is how you saw it.

What do both of these illustrations have in common? They both imply that letter and word reversals are examples of unusual behavior. They imply that something is wrong with these students. Finally, they imply that something is preventing these students from seeing correctly. For why else would they see backwards?

Do students really see backwards? What should a parent do when told by the school they suspect their child has a perceptual disorder?

The answer is: do not panic!

Too much has been made of letter and number reversals. They are as common and unwelcome as the chicken pox. They are normal; every young child has them.

What Causes Letter and Number Reversals?

What feelings do you imagine when I say "ice cream cone?" Can you almost taste one, or feel its coolness, or do you remember an event you can associate with an ice cream cone? Do the same with the words "roller coaster." How does your stomach feel? Do you see the roller coaster in your mind? Where are you mentally? Who is with you? This activity isn't hard is it? You are able to imagine the ice cream cone or the roller coaster.

Now let us try the same activity. But this time, I want you to think of the letter "b." Tell me, what do you feel? What images of taste or touch or personal experience can you conjure up over the letter "b"?

The answer is nothing!

Letters are an Abstraction

Letters are an abstraction. They have no intrinsic value. They have no purpose other than representing. They cannot be experienced, manipulated, or enjoyed like an ice cream cone or a roller coaster ride. Students, therefore, have to be taught their value and how to interpret them.

Interpreting letters (especially lowercase) is initially based on the ability to hold these letters constant in space. Letters are composed of four line shapes: the vertical, diagonal, horizontal, and curved. Different combinations of these shapes form the twenty-six letters of the alphabet.

Spatial Orientation is the Key

Spatial orientation is the key to letter differentiation. And spatial orientation is dependent upon an adequate mastery of key directional words.

Consider the following: imagine you get confused with left and right. Sometimes you use the terms correctly and other times you do not. For example, the chances are fifty-fifty that you will use them correctly, even if you do not know your right from your left. "Ok" you say, "so I don't know my left from my right. Big deal, what does that have to do with reversals?" It has everything to do with it.

Adequate Understanding of Left and Right

The only difference between a lowercase "b" and a lower case "d," "p," or "q" is that the circle is on either the left or the right of the vertical line. Going a step further, different letter combinations are used to form words. Each combination is dependent upon an adequate understanding of left and right.

When you confuse left from right you are going to have difficulty visually discriminating words that are dependent upon such knowledge. For example, the only difference between "was" and "saw" is based on where you start reading. If you start reading from right to left, it will be one word. If you start reading from left to right it will be another word. So, if you confuse left and right, you will reverse. Is it because you see backwards? No. You are not seeing backwards. It's just that you still do not know your left from your right; and because of this, you forget where to start. One day you read right to left, the next day left to right. You lack a consistent frame of reference.

What do Reversals Indicate?

What do reversals indicate? Probably not very much. While severe and pronounced reversals can be a cause of concern in students in the middle and upper grades, they are very common in the early grades. Young children frequently reverse numbers or letters. Remember: children reverse because they confuse left from right. They don't see backwards.

Do reversals indicate a perceptual disorder? In most instances, the answer is no. Young children who reverse are not suffering from a crippling perceptual illness. Too often, such a comparison is made. This is wrong. These children are not ill. There is no evidence to support the assumption they are any different from their non-reversing peers. Left-right awareness is based on the student's developmental "time clock." This awareness is housed in the parietal-occipital region of the brain. It appears that this area becomes active somewhere between 5-8 years of age.

Sensation Versus Perception

The reason why many subscribe to the notion of impairment lies in the failure to distinguish between two terms: sensation and perception. These terms are not the same.

The senses are nothing more than mechanical receptors designed to transmit particular forms of energy to the brain for processing. Each sense is energy specific. The type of energy decides which sense is to be used. For example, if the energy source is light, the eyes will be used. If the energy source is sound, the ears will be used. The senses do not process these energy forms. They simply act as energy conduits—pathways so to speak. They provide a vehicle for these energy forms to reach the brain for processing.

Perception is a Cognitive Process

Perception involves the interpretation of energy forms. It is a cognitive process. It is what happens after energy forms have been delivered to the brain by the senses. It requires thinking.

Perception is the process in which meaning is given to these energy forms. We sort them out. We label them. We give them names. Perception provides this opportunity for meaning.

Perception is not objective. Perception is highly subjective and dependent upon many factors such as age, sex, and life experience. While two people might experience the same thing (an act of sensation), they might interpret it quite differently (an act of perception). It is the basis for a difference of opinion.

Sensory Versus Perceptual Impairments

Sensory difficulties and perceptual difficulties are also not the same. A child who has injured his eye and is prevented from seeing letters on a chalkboard is experiencing a sensory impairment. A child who recognizes that there are two letters written on the chalkboard but cannot tell you the difference between these two letters (such as "b" and "d") has no sensory impairment. The difficulty is in processing. Yes, he is having difficulty recognizing these letters, however, he is not physically seeing backwards.

Frank Smith, internationally known author and educational reformer, wrote years ago in his book, *Reading Without Nonsense* (1979):

> It is completely nonsensical to say that seeing backwards causes reversals. Seeing backwards is a logical and physical impossibility. It is physically impossible to see part of our field of view one way and the rest the other—to see two cars going one way and one in the reverse direction when they are all in fact heading the same way.
>
> A child who sees a letter backwards would have to see everything else backwards at the same time, including the paper or board on which the letter was written. However, it is logically impossible for everything to be seen backwards, because each element, and paradoxically therefore everything, would still appear to be the right way round. (p.153)

This information is as valuable today as it was a quarter of a century ago. Yet, twenty-five years later, parents and teachers are still presented with experts who stress a reading disorder based on "visual impairments" and justified by letter reversals. This simply is not true. Let me state it again. Letter and number reversals are perfectly normal and do not cause reading failure. They can be easily treated.

Why do some students reverse more than others? As I have already mentioned, part of the answer has to do with maturation and experience. A bigger part of the answer as we shall see later has to do with the concept of material inappropriateness. At this point, it is just important to note that it is not because of an innate disability. An innate disability does not cause failing students to see backwards.

Intellectual Deficits

The following is a letter given to me by a parent. The letter, written by her daughter, reads as follows: (Note: the parentheses with the spelling corrections are mine.)

"Once upon a time a little girl how (who) was in the fourth grade had no friends at all. She just walked around at resevse (recess) and did nothing at all. In reading she was in the lowest reading group and everyone called her names in homeroom. In math she was in the top math group and they seed (said) she did not need to be in that class. In homeroom she could not read the words on the page. She has a reading disabelite (disability) and cannot ear (hear) the sounds in words. Her name is…and she needs friends. If you are wondering what she is like call…or the home number is…She needs friends call today."

Imagine the pain this little girl is feeling. Imagine also the grief her parents are experiencing. The girl has no friends. She is made fun of, ridiculed, and shunned by her peers. Why?

An Important Conversation with Parents at a Complete Loss

Much of the answer to "Why?" is contained in a conversation I had while I was teaching in an elementary grade school. The conversation was with the parents of a seven-year-old boy. The boy was not doing well in school. He was in the second grade and a non-reader. The parents were asked to come to school for a conference to discuss the situation.

The family lived in an affluent upper-class community outside a major northeastern urban area. Both parents were college graduates.

"We're at a complete loss," said the boy's father. "When we talk to Billy he sounds so bright. Our friends have always commented on how bright he appears. And that's why we're so puzzled," his father continued. "He looks so bright and he acts so bright and yet we all know he's retarded!"

Billy was not retarded. In fact, his I.Q. was above average. Why then did his parents think he was retarded?

Billy's parents thought he was retarded because he could not read and as they put it: "Everyone knows if you can't read, you must be retarded."

Nothing could be farther from the truth. Too often, reading ability is equated with intelligence. Only the brightest can read successfully is the assumption. Those who cannot read must be cognitively limited. This is absolutely incorrect as the following example illustrates.

I was once asked, as a school psychologist, to perform an educational evaluation on a 16-year-old high school girl. Included in the evaluation was a reading assessment. I first asked the girl to read a series of words that increased in complexity. The words ranged from first grade level through high school. The girl did beautifully. She read the entire list without error.

The evaluation took place in a library reference room. Included in this room were college level texts, encyclopedias, and other standard reference texts. I randomly selected a college level text, which dealt with the life and times of Winston Churchill. I opened to the middle of the text and asked her to read. Again, she read every word correctly. There was not a single error.

Anyone listening to the girl read orally could easily conclude she was an excellent reader. She never missed a single word. She read without error. Not one single mistake. It was perfect.

She also did not understand anything she read.

What people could not have possibly guessed was that this excellent reader was mentally handicapped with an I.Q. well under 50. The girl was a word caller and suffered from a condition known as "developmental hyperlexia." It appears that for whatever the reason, this girl was born with the ability to recognize words of any length or complexity. She was not taught this skill. It just occurred (usually before age five). Sadly, this skill occurred in the world of a cognitively challenged client. So, while this young girl could identify almost any word, she lacked the cognitively ability to process its meaning. The meanings of words were and always will be beyond her comprehension.

Notion Laid to Rest

The relationship between learning to read and intelligence is not a strong one. It is a double-edged sword. While we can have cognitively limited students reading words at any standard, we also have many bright students who are not even remotely close to reading up to their potential. They are not cognitively limited. They are capable of comprehending at much higher levels. Unfortunately, these students see themselves as dumb or stupid. This is wrong. They are very bright students who are in critical need of a major reading attitude adjustment.

What do I mean by "reading attitude adjustment" and why is it so important? The answer centers on one of the most time-tested philosophies in the history of reading instruction. The application of this philosophy is crucial to future reading success. More importantly, when this philosophy is overlooked (or worse, not believed) the results will be complete and total student reading failure—regardless of age or potential.

What is the name of this critical philosophy for student reading success? I call it "The Little Train Theory." Yes, that's right, the story we read as kids in kindergarten about that tiny little train who needed to believe that "it could"—in order to pull that heavy load up and over the huge mountain—is the very same philosophy that can make all the difference for future reading success. Quite simply, students who think they can succeed, will succeed—regardless of age, race, label, or economic background. Those, who do not believe, will fail.

Sadly, too many bright students, who once started school believing they could, do not believe it anymore. They have given up. They have become firm members of the "I can't do this" camp. This "I can't" membership cuts across all grades. It is the most frustrating and debilitating by-product of pronounced reading failure. The more they fail, the stronger they believe that "they can't," as the following examples illustrate.

Over the past thirty years, I have traveled the nation giving reading demonstrations to parents and teachers of non-readers. My travels have taken me from inner city schools to rural schools to at-risk adolescent treatment facilities to maximum-security prisons to the lobbies of state legislatures and offices of state commissioners and superintendents of education. I have been in schools in the north, south, east and west. I have worked with elementary, middle, high school and adult students.

My demonstration is always given under one condition. I will only work with the worst student they have. In other words, I did not want the marginal or somewhat poor reader. I wanted the "I'm pulling my hair out, this kid is driving me crazy" reader. I did not want those "struggling readers" testing merely at the twentieth percentile. I wanted those students stranded at "ground zero" (testing at the zero percentile). I wanted the non-reader.

Prior reading ability or label was of no concern to me. I didn't care if they were rich, poor, white, black, dyslexic, limited English, learning disabled, cognitively handicapped, hearing impaired, emotionally disturbed, mildly autistic, incarcerated or at-risk. I expected them to experience an immediate age-appropriate reading experience. In other words, I stated that these non-readers would be able to experience what it felt like to read an age-appropriate passage fluently, with full comprehension, within the first thirty-minute diagnostic lesson.

As you can imagine, some viewed my claim as outrageous, impossible, and even foolish. One major reading association failed to advertise my first book, *The Thirty Minute Cure, How to Teach Anyone to Read in Thirty Minutes or Less.* Yet, after over 1000 demos given over these thirty years, I have never failed to meet my promise. The reason why my demonstration works will be discussed in later chapters. What I want to discuss now is the dramatic change in student attitude observed before and after one particular demonstration.

Success is Not Enough

It is important to note, that most educators do recognize the importance of success. In fact, all reading specialists are trained to diagnose failing readers at three key levels of instruction: independent reading ability, instructional reading ability and frustration reading ability. These levels are based on the assessment of a student's actual reading performance while reading graded reading passages of 100 words. These passages are graded for complexity and are identified as first grade, second grade, third grade and so on.

For example, a student who could read a passage with 95% or higher accuracy from first grade passages would be classified as reading independently at the first grade level. Those testing at 94-86% accuracy from second grade passages would be classified as reading at a second grade independent level. Those testing at 85% accuracy or below from third grade passages would be classified as having a third grade frustration level. Teachers are taught to use these levels to place their students in appropriate instructional reading books and materials.

In our previous example, the student testing at first grade would be asked to read independently from books written at the first grade or below. He would be taught instructionally from second grade books and below. And he would be kept away from any written material third grade level or higher for fear that this would be too difficult and only serve to frustrate him even more. Like it or not, a "reading achievement" ceiling has been set. Potential has been limited.

The above mentioned independent, instructional and frustration reading assessment is the cornerstone of our nation's reading assessment system. It is taught in every teacher preparation college across the nation. Reading teachers cannot graduate without it. However, there is a problem with this model. It does not work for non-readers—especially those trapped in grade three and higher!

In fact, the higher the grade level, the more damaging this assessment model becomes. By middle and high school, this "model" actually becomes life threatening. Why? Because it clearly underestimates student potential and assumes they cannot go higher.

In addition, it destroys the reading attitude of non-readers. Even worse, it actually causes many to give up on themselves. In other words, what confidence can be gained by placing a fourteen-year-old streetwise non-reader (where image is everything) in first grade material that smacks of dancing bears and bunny rabbits?

Finally, if you think non-readers don't notice or don't underestimate their own potential, you are quite mistaken. The following examples illustrate what I have encountered over and over pertaining to the poor reading self-esteem of our nation's non-readers. They simply no longer believe in themselves.

Case Study: Exposing Special Education's "Dirty little secret"

Bronx, New York

Raul* is an African-American / Latino student in the ninth grade living in the Bronx in New York City. He has been in special education classes for the past four years with no noticeable growth or improvement. He is still testing as a virtual non-reader. Raul is a classic example of what I call a "Special Education Lifer."

Allow me, as a former special education teacher, special education director and school psychologist, to share with you what I call special education's "dirty little secret." While recognized behind closed doors, very few publicly acknowledge this secret. The secret is that when it comes to students with a hardcore reading disability (e.g. real life "non-readers"), special education does not know what to do with them anymore than regular education does.

That is right, after 30 years and close to a third of a trillion dollars of federal funds alone, special education is still failing to impact significant numbers of identified non-readers. In fact, as Raul illustrates, little or no growth is not uncommon even after years and years and years of receiving special education services! These non-readers have received "a special education life sentence"—once enrolled in special education, they never get out. Even worse, the gap between their reading potential (as measured by their IQ) and actual reading ability (as measured by their reading scores) actually becomes larger and larger over the years.

According to Raul's records, he was classified as Learning Disabled and a virtual non-reader. He entered special education four years before. His independent reading level four years ago was first grade. Now, after

* Name has been changed

fours years and hundreds and hundreds of instructional hours later, he is still reading independently at first grade. No change was made.

At Their Wits End

Let me make this clear, it was not because the district did not care about Raul. In fact, it was just the opposite. Raul was a high priority for the district. They wanted to help him badly. He was assigned to one of their best teachers. They used nationally recognized methods and materials. Still no change. No impact. The district team was at their wits end. In other districts, some might say, "Raul is just one of those kids who will never learn to read, no matter what we do." (Yes, they really do say this behind closed doors).

It is interesting to note that this "blame the victim" philosophy is not unusual. Hundreds of thousands of kids have been unofficially given up on. Their teachers have thrown in the "instructional towel" and are spending more time making institutional accommodations (such as alternative degrees and the lowering of standards) than eliminating the reading gap. They know these students are free falling in failure and they are just trying to soften (what they see) as the inevitable blow.

The "blame the victim" philosophy is real. It happens. I believe it is caused purely by human nature. Let's face it; teachers are no different from their students. They do not want to fail or be seen as failures—especially when they are doing a pretty good job reaching most of their poor and struggling readers. MOST-but not all of their students.

Imagine you are a hard working, dedicated special education teacher. You are reaching most of your students. Yet, you have a hard-core number of students who have literally defied everything you have tried. You are working longer and harder with them and seeing little or no results. You know in your heart of hearts that you are a good teacher and yet, you are failing to reach them.

Isn't it just human nature to shift the blame off your shoulders and onto the student? "It's not me! It can't be me! Why look at what I'm doing with all the others! I am successful. It has to be these students, their parents, or the system in general. They are not ready. They haven't been taught. They're poor or don't speak English or have below average intelligence or…. It's not me! Anybody but me."

Lack of Readiness

At one point in time everyone in the education industry has heard a colleague utter the phrase "not ready for a formal education," when referring to a particular student. Schools have used "lack of readiness" or "at-risk" for years to identify or label children who they believe are earmarked for potential school failure because they lack the skills necessary for school success. What do we really know about "readiness"? What does readiness consist of? More importantly, is a lack of readiness a good predictor of future academic achievement?

Please remember: readiness is a relative term that means different things to different people. For example, I began my applied research work with non-readers when I was on the graduate faculty of a major university. Through my research and experiences with at-risk and special education students, I developed a new approach to teaching reading to the students caught in the "bottom of the bottom" percentiles. (I will delve into what my new approach became and is later in the book). I decided to try my new approach on students identified as at-risk. Research has shown that certain students are more vulnerable toward future failure. They are at a greater risk. More importantly, tests had been developed to identify these students during their preschool years. Generally speaking, these students are low income, minority and limited in English.

At-risk Students

My initial research included a group of students identified by a nationally recognized test as "at-risk." This test compared these students to other students their age who took the same test under similar conditions across the nation. The test produced a score for readiness. Students who scored above this number were considered ready for school. Students who fell below this number were considered not ready. Yes, the vast majority of students in my study were poor, minority and came from homes where parents did not have a great deal of formal education. Standard English was not used frequently.

A score of 88 or below was the test's cut-off point for readiness. Students who scored below 88 were considered at-risk. This meant the chances were very good these students would fail grades, do poorly in academics, need special services, and probably drop out of school.

Dramatic Success

I decided to go even lower than 88. I only took students with scores of 50 and below. According to the test, students who scored this low were the absolute bottom of the bottom. They would not be considered ready for a formal school experience, and according to their results, they certainly were not ready to read.

Guess what happened...

When I began using my new reading approach, I wanted to see its impact on those students who were considered among the neediest. I started out with 18 at-risk students in the program. The results were fantastic. At the end of the year, teacher observation and testing indicated all were functioning as well as their achieving classmates. All 18 went into regular second grade. Only one student required special education.

I was able to follow these students at four and nine year intervals. The results were even more exciting. Fifteen students remained in the original school district (three moved out of the district). All fifteen were still in school. No one had quit. Better yet, 80% had never failed a grade. Even better than that, 40% of these kids never had grades below 80's and 90's throughout their school careers. Not bad for a group of not-ready, at-risk kids.

Thirty years and almost 80 studies involving over 8,000 students classified as at-risk still reinforce the notion that all students can experience an immediate and successful reading experience regardless of prior background and reading ability. This notion is the backbone of the No Child Left Behind legislation—particularly as it pertains to four national at-risk subgroups: low income, limited English, special education, and minority and especially those testing in these groups at the zero to fifteenth percentile range.

Don't Blame Lack of Readiness

While I know good teachers and administrators are frustrated in trying to meet the reading needs of over 440,000 non-readers in our schools, they have to absolutely avoid taking the easiest way out, mainly blaming the victim and/or their parents or current life circumstances.

Generally speaking, I believe non-readers already come to school with the prerequisites for learning to read. Even more exciting, non-readers can have an immediate and successful grade level reading experience commensurate with their cognitive capacity.

What do I mean by commensurate with their cognitive capacity? I mean that we cannot ignore real cognitive or physical limitations. Sadly, there are brain-injured students who are and always will be limited. They operate at a much lower level—more like much younger children. For example, we cannot expect adolescent and adult clients with severe cognitive restrictions (IQ's 40 and below) to read high school material. They cannot do it, no matter how hard we try.

However, nothing stops us from teaching brain-injured students to read at their developmental age. We have seen older clients with IQ's as low as 30 reading fluently with comprehension from material suitable to their developmental age.

Fortunately, special educators call the population "low incidence" because they are very low in number. Even better, they are not among the 440,000 non-readers (or the millions of students testing in reading comprehension at the 0–15 reading percentile) I will now discuss. As for this latter group, being able to read fluently from age-appropriate, grade level material is not only possible, it is fully expected. As our experience with Raul will continue to demonstrate…

Behind His Friends

The special education team was correct. Raul could not read fluently above the first grade. Even worse, he knew it. Raul stated to me and in front of the teachers and administrators in the group that he was a poor reader. He told me that reading was very hard for him. He knew he was years behind his friends. You could see that while he volunteered to do the demonstration with me, he was clearly embarrassed about his reading ability and hardly made eye contact. His head drooped.

The special education team in the room was also very concerned. While they wanted to believe there might be a new way to reach Raul, I could see that they really did not believe it could happen. More importantly, they were feeling Raul's embarrassment and fear that he was going to fail at reading yet again.

Tension was high. You could cut it with a knife. It got even higher when they saw the level of reading material I put in front of Raul. The look of shock was amazing. Quite frankly, I think they thought they had made a huge mistake by placing Raul in the hands of a mad man. There was no way Raul could work at this level. I could see the thoughts going through their heads, "No way! This man was nuts. What have we gotten ourselves into? How can we get him to leave?"

There was no way I was leaving the room. Actually, I was used to this reaction. It happens everywhere I go. Especially when I placed the following five words in front of a non-reader like Raul: attorney, acquaintance, astounded, abundant, and accommodate! I smiled at the look of absolute horror that I saw on the team's faces. It turned even worse after Raul told me that he couldn't read even one of these words. Raul told me that the passage I showed him, using all of those words, was: "Too hard! I can't do this," he said.

Thirty minutes later, Raul was reading aloud, to the group, the following passage:

"The attorney and her acquaintance were astounded at the abundant size of the rock singer's house. The house was able to accommodate over a hundred people."

Raul's fluency was excellent. He was able to read the passage and recognize each word, both in and out of context. He also gave a meaningful definition for each. In other words, when I showed Raul the word "attorney" on a flash card, he could now tell me the word and that the word meant "lawyer." Raul did the same with "acquaintance" (Raul said "a friend"), "astounded" (Raul said it means, "To be surprised"), "abundant" (Raul said, "To have lots of something"), and "accommodate" (Raul's definition was "To make room").

Dramatic Change in Attitude

The best thing now about Raul was his visible change in attitude. It was dramatic. His head was held high. His eyes glistened. His smile was overpowering, especially when Raul told the group that the passage that he identified just thirty minutes ago as being "too hard" was now "too easy!" Raul was now starting to become a believer. He could do faster, higher and more. But even he was not fully convinced of how high he could go as the following dialogue between Raul and myself illustrates.

The dialogue began with a simple question to Raul:

Me: Raul, do you know what grade level this passage is?
Raul: No.
Me: Take a guess.
Raul: Fourth Grade?
Me: No. Guess again.
Raul: Third?
Me: No. Guess again.
Raul: Second?

Please note that Raul's response is typical of what I get from almost every non-reader who participates in this dialogue. It is typical of the "I can't" attitude that non-readers have built into their system. First, they generally start at a grade very far below their actual grade. In this example, Raul's estimate started five full grade levels below his actual grade. Five full grade levels!

Second, when I ask them to guess again, they almost always guess lower. They truly cannot believe they could go higher. It simply is not in their current mind set. Watch what happens to Raul as I tell him to go higher!

Me: No. That's not the grade level. Try higher.
Raul: Higher? (Raul now has a look of astonishment on his face)
Me: Yes, Higher!
Raul: Fifth?
Me: No. Go higher.
Raul: Sixth? (I can see Raul's not really sure)
Me: No, go higher.
Raul: Ninth?! (Raul says with a huge smile)
Me: Yes. It's eighth to ninth grade material! Tell me. Who just read ninth grade material?
Raul: I did! (Raul is just beaming.)

The change in Raul is now complete. He has experienced grade level reading for the first time in his life—not merely recognizing words but reading fluently with full comprehension. Is he cured? Absolutely not. But, he is on his way to a full recovery. Raul can't wait to continue. He is now a believer going from "I can't" to "I did!" And that, according to the "Little Train Theory," is half the battle.

The Next Inevitable Question

The special education team could not believe what they saw. Raul's performance astounded them. I now awaited the arrival of what my experience has taught me will be the next inevitable question.

It didn't take long to arrive. "What Raul did was truly amazing but how do we know it's not a trick?"

"What about long term memory? In other words, will Raul remember how to read this passage with fluency and comprehension a day or a week later?"

"Absolutely," I enthusiastically replied.

"Raul will not forget because it was taught to him in a way that guarantees full fluency and comprehension," I said. "Students just don't fail when this approach is used. I've seen this same change in attitude over and over. That is why I call my new approach 'failure free'." I continued by stating that I would call them back in a week. "Give it to him one week later. Tell me how he did."

One week later, I called. Raul didn't forget a word thanks to my new "failure free" approach. As I have already mentioned, how my "failure free" approach works will be explained later. What is currently important is that we are accomplishing this success over and over again across the nation with the students in greatest need—non-readers—regardless of age, label or location. More importantly, although they might not be ready to learn through a traditional reading approach, they are nonetheless ready to learn to read with full fluency and comprehension through the Failure Free Reading Methodology. This book provides the insight into this new corrective reading action. The time has come to stop giving up on these failing students. We must stop looking for excuses to justify why they are failing.

Non-readers do not need to fail. Not a single one. Why not? Because anyone (and I do mean anyone) within a very broad range of intelligence can learn to read fluently with full comprehension from age-appropriate material. Quickly. Easily.

So what do non-readers really need? Non-readers need to be given an opportunity to show what they can do—regardless of their race, background, gender and socioeconomic status. We have the ability to wipe reading failure off the face of the earth. The opportunity is here, and I dare anyone to prove me wrong.

Were These Teachers Wrong?

How can I make such a bold assumption? Because I have seen reading failure eliminated time and time again using my "failure free" approach. I have seen students whose teachers say, "they cannot read," read immediately, fluently, and with full comprehension at least two to three grade levels higher than ever expected.

Were these teachers wrong? No, they weren't. These students really could not read in their classroom. They did stutter and stop. They never read fluently a day in their life. They couldn't recognize words or read with any semblance of comprehension. The problem, as you shall soon see, was not within them. The problem was without. The problem was within the materials and the approach—not the teachers, and certainly not the students.

Failure Free Reading Case Study:
Fairland East Elementary's After-School Solution

RESEARCH QUESTIONS
Ohio Proficiency Test:

Is it possible to accelerate the learning curve of 4th grade at-risk and special education students in a 4-week treatment period as measured by the Ohio Proficiency Test?

Can this impact be demonstrated with students below the 40th percentile?

Star Reading Assessment

Do these results transfer to other nationally standardized measuring instruments, such as STAR Reading?

High Impact Tutorial Assistance

Can this treatment be implemented in a tutorial setting utilizing certified and non-certified tutors?- (e.g. OhioReads)

SETTING
Southeastern Ohio School located in the Appalachian region

At-risk and special education students were taught by teachers, tutors, and volunteers in an after school setting using OhioReads funds

POPULATION
Failure Free Reading Treatment Group: 72

4th grade at-risk and special education students in need of tutorial assistance who were able to participate in after school program

Control Group: 15

4th grade at-risk and special education students from the same school, with comparable academic achievement, but were unable to attend after school tutorial

AMOUNT OF TRAINING
(1) 3-hour introductory session
1 follow up visitation

LENGTH OF INSTRUCTIONAL TIME
18 days
Mondays-Thursdays: OhioReads after school tutorials

OHIO PROFICIENCY RESULTS
Failure Free ReadingTreatment Group: 62
4th grade at-risk and special education students who had both Pre Test
    and Post test scores for the Ohio Proficiency Test

Control Group: 13
4th grade at-risk and special education students who had both Pre Test
    and Post Test scores for the Ohio Proficiency Test

RESULTS
Failure Free ReadingTreatment Group (N=62)
83% of all students showed growth from Riverside* (Pre Test) to 4th
    Grade Proficiency (Post Test)

Control Group (N=13)
38% of all students showed growth from Riverside* (Pre Test) to 4th
    Grade Proficiency (Post Test)
*A 3rd grade, off year, Proficiency Test

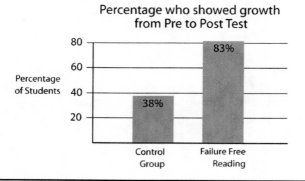

Percentage who showed growth from Pre to Post Test

Failure Free Reading Treatment Group (N=62)

<u>8.62</u> Change in average score from Riverside Pre Test (x pre= 209.08) to 4th Grade Proficiency Post Test (x post=217.70)

Control Group (N=13)*

<u>-2.31</u> Average difference from Riverside Pre Test (x post=213.00)

*Students who took both Riverside (3rd Grade, off year, proficiency Test) and 4th Grade Ohio Proficiency Test

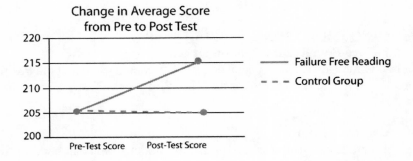

POPULATIONS
Failure Free ReadingTreatment Group

48 Treatment Students who failed the Proficiency Pre Test

Control Group

9 Control Students who failed the Proficiency Pre Test

<u>RESULTS</u>
Failure Free ReadingTreatment Group (N-48)

<u>77%</u> of all students failing Riverside (Pre Test) actually passed 4th Grade Proficiency (Post Test)

Control Group (N=9)

<u>22%</u> of all students failing Riverside (Pre Test) actually passed 4th Grade Proficiency

(Post Test)

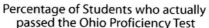

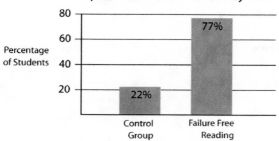

Failure Free ReadingTreatment Group (N=48)

<u>9.30</u> Change in average score from Riverside Pre Test (x pre = 206.34) to 4th Grade Proficiency Post Test (x post = 215.64)

Control Group (N=9)*

<u>-0.72</u> Change in average score from Riverside Pre Test (x pre = 206.29) to 4th Grade Proficiency Post Test (x post = 205.57)

*Students who took both Riverside (3rd Grade, off-year, proficiency Test) and 4th Grade Ohio Proficiency Test

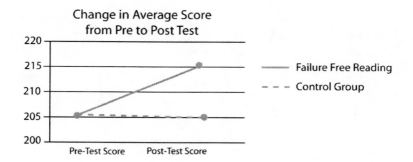

<u>STAR READING ASSESSMENT RESULTS</u>
<u>POPULATION</u>
(Students testing below 40th percentile)
Failure Free Reading Treatment Group <u>29</u>

Of the 72 Students in the entire treatment group, 29 had Pre Test reading scores below the 40th percentile (as measured by STAR reading Assessment)

Control Group 15
Students in the control group had Pre Test reading scores below the 40th percentile (as measured by STAR Reading Assessment)

RESULTS
Failure Free ReadingTreatment Group (N=29)
8.2 Months growth in reading from STAR Pre Test (x pre = 3.02) to STAR Post Test (x post = 3.84)

Control Group (N=15)
4.8 Months growth in reading from STAR Pre Test (x pre = 3.26) to STAR Post Test (x post = 3.74)

Change in Average Grade Level
Equivalence Score from STAR Pre Test to Post Test

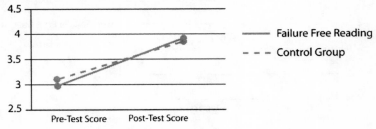

Failure Free ReadingTreatment Group (N=29)

<u>12.68%</u> the average percentile growth from Pre to Post Test on the STAR Reading Assessment.

Control Group (N=15)

<u>5.76%</u> The average percentile growth from Pre to Post Test on the STAR Reading Assessment.

Average Percentile Growth from Pre to Post Test

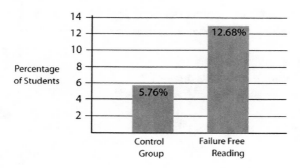

IN CONCLUSION
HIGH IMPACT TUTORIAL ASSISTANCE

All of these dramatic results were <u>achieved after only 18 days</u> of tutorial assistance from certified and non-certified tutors participating in the OhioReads Grant.

Chapter 2

What Really Causes Reading Failure?

What do the following numbers represent?

8 Million
3 Thousand
40 Percent
25 Times

The answers compiled by researchers in a report to the Carnegie Corporation of New York, *Reading Next: A Vision for Action and Research in Middle and High School Literacy* (2004) will astound you.

8 Million. This represents the number of students in grades 4–12 who cannot comprehend grade level reading material. Can you believe it? Eight million students who are testing significantly below grade level in reading comprehension. These students are on a fast track to nowhere. As one Detroit judge put it, "if you can't read in our society, you have two choices: welfare or crime. Sadly, in some circles, crime has the greater status."

3 Thousand. This is the number of students who are dropping out of school each day. Most are non-readers. That is 600 students dying every instructional hour or 10 students heading out the door every instructional minute. Can you believe that we are creating such an environment of failure? Forget the notion of pre-school and early childhood long term fixes. We are hemorrhaging in the middle and high school grades. These students need help now!

We cannot wait ten to twelve more years. Heck, we can't wait ten to twelve more days while an additional 36,000 students drop out of school. We need to save these high school students now. They are in need of immediate triage therapy. We need to stop their bleeding immediately. Fortunately, this can be done.

40 Percent. This is the average number of African-American and Latino students who will not graduate on time or with a regular high school diploma. This is just the average. In some inner cities, this number is closer to 70 and 80 percent. Can you imagine? Why? Because most cannot read even remotely close to their actual grade level—often, after years of remedial instruction.

25 Times. This is the likelihood that non-readers and high school students testing well below the twentieth percentile will drop out of school. That's right. Non-readers and lowest performing readers are 25 times or 2500% more likely to drop out of school than their grade level achieving peers.

To say that in the United States of America we have a literacy crisis of epidemic proportions is an understatement. Sadly, and all too often, we turn to a quick fix or to what sounds good on a 9-second TV sound bite. We latch onto slogans such as "all students can learn" even though most teachers really do not believe it. For those students that don't learn, they go out the door or get shelved in a program waiting until the day they are old enough to officially drop out.

Even worse, is a tendency to ignore the present and look to the future. We set new national reading commissions every decade. These commissions then talk about new research based preventative measures that, if taken, will provide real long-term fixes such as, "All students will read on grade level by third grade." We are told repeatedly that if we put the money on what really works for our first graders, then we will truly eliminate illiteracy within the next decade. We've spent the money, boy, have we spent the money!

I wish I had one cent for every dollar spent on the "proven reading research practice of the day" over the past three decades alone. The money I would receive would be enormous, especially if you consider that at least a quarter of a trillion dollars has been spent in federal aid alone. Double that, if you factor in the additional money spent in special education funds. Let's see, one cent on $500,000,000,000. Ummm? Donald Trump would have to move aside. There would really be a new rich kid on his block. But, back to reality…

Over the past thirty years, I have personally experienced (as either a teacher, an administrator, professor or businessman) the impact created by at least three different national reading commissions. I have heard dramatic predictions from each. Thirty years later, in the education field, I have been able to see how fruitless many of these assumptions really were.

Scores No Higher

For example, the National Center for Educational Statistics recently announced that the average reading scores of thirteen-year-old students across the nation in 2004 were no higher than the average reading scores of similar students in 1999. In other words, five years of pronounced reading research based reform (coupled with billions of dollars in federal assistance for low performing schools) has produced no significant increase in middle school reading performance. None whatsoever.

The results were even worse for seventeen year olds. The National Center for Educational Statistics found that when it comes to the performance of seventeen year olds there was no significant difference in reading comprehension scores in 2004 and those scores found in 1971!

In other words, after 33 years of promises, money and active reform, nothing happened. In fact, things have gotten worse.

Where are those leading researchers of the seventies, of the eighties, or even the early nineties who promised they could produce significant change and wipe out illiteracy in all grades if we only put our funds in the early grades on research based reading programs that they claimed could not fail? Well, fail they did.

Pity the poor students who failed and dropped out of school or ended up in useless special education programs over the past thirty-three years because of these false claims. They made these students and their parents promises that they did not live up to, and it just isn't right.

One Word that Seems Above Reproach

How can they justify this? It's not hard. As I mentioned, these commissions (and to a lesser extent gullible politicians) always use one word that seems above reproach to justify these foolish decisions. One word demonstrates their intentions are both honorable and smart. What is that word they use to quiet the critics and march helplessly forward? **Research.**

"We'll only do what the research says to do," say many lawmakers. "We'll convene a National Reading Panel. We'll bring in the experts."

Why the experts?

"Because the experts are objective and deal only in fact," they say. "These experts couldn't possibly have hidden agendas. The best and the brightest will lead the way. They will provide the straightest and most direct unbiased path to full literacy."

Right? No. This is wrong—way, way wrong.

Researchers Are No Different

The truth is that researchers are no different from any other special interest group. They do have bias. They do support different positions and they do set up research designs that lend support to those positions. This is especially true in research pertaining to the teaching of reading.

The reasons why bias exists are many, and I will discuss some of them shortly. However, it is important to know that when it comes to research pertaining to teaching reading, there are really only three reading research facts that anyone needs to know.

These three facts are universally accepted and 100% accurate. Absolutely no one can argue with these three critical reading research facts. Absolutely no one. Once known, real common sense educational decisions can be made immediately to affect those groups who are currently failing and whose educational needs are being ignored or unmet.

So let us look at these three critical facts and begin the process of saving the lives of those students in our society who need our help the most. Together we can make a huge difference.

Three Basic Reading Research Facts

Reading is the most researched topic in education. Thousands of articles have been written and billions upon billions of dollars have been spent determining the best reading approach. Yet, if I had to summarize all of this research into one statement that you could take to the bank it would say:

1. All reading programs work!

Whether it's phonics, sight, linguistic, whole language, or language experience, one thing is certain, every one of these programs work. They all work. They won't let you down. You can rest easy knowing that you have just picked a winning program. No doubt about it. Case closed.

How do I know these programs work? I know because research has documented their effectiveness. They exist because these approaches have stood the test of time. I can cite you case after case. I can give you the names of hundreds of districts, thousands of schools and millions of students who have benefited from every approach mentioned. It is why each approach has so many proponents. It is also why the proponents are so full of passion and why the debate never cools on any side. They are satisfied customers.

The proponents have no trouble singing the praises of their approach because their approach works for them. They are sold on it. It is why we have phonics advocates, whole language advocates, or language experience advocates, because it has worked for each of them respectively.

It is also the reason why there is so much confusion about which program to use. They're all good. They all have people who swear by them. They all get the job done.

What exactly do I mean by getting the job done? More importantly, how can I say they all work? Didn't I just spend page after page bemoaning how bad things are in the teaching of reading?

Yes, you are right on all counts. It appears we have a problem. In other words, if these programs all work, why do we hear such terrible things about the problem of illiteracy in our society? Why? Because of the second most important reading research fact, namely:

2. No reading program is 100% effective!

You see, even though **all reading programs work, they don't work for all students.** There is no reading program available today that is 100% effective for all students in all situations. How do I know this? I know this because I spent the past thirty years of my life seeking a "fail safe" reading solution that works for all.

I read the research. I searched the literature. I met the experts. When it was all over, I came to the following conclusion: a 100% effective reading solution for all students of all ages simply does not exist. Nada. Zip. Niet. No way. Quit looking. Don't waste your time. Been there. Done that.

The truth is that I've tried almost every known reading approach from neurological impress to structured phonics, to basal readers, to whole language, to language experience. I've tried auditory approaches, visual approaches, and tactile/kinesthetic approaches. I've analyzed and synthesized, story charted, traced wooden letters with eyes open and blindfolded, as well as drawn letters in the sand, on students' backs and in the air.

If that's not enough, I also spent eight years of my life as a school administrator spending the taxpayer's money on methods and materials specifically designed for struggling non-readers. I listened to the sales presentations, heard the testimonials, visited the programs, talked to the teachers and administrators, and met the authors. Do you know what I found? Every one of these programs, approaches and materials worked. That's right, they all worked! Unfortunately, these programs do not work for every student. This brings me to the third critical fact:

3.   All reading programs produce failure!

That's right! There are limitations contained in every known successful reading approach and program. Even worse, some of the most successful programs are down right harmful when applied to all. In other words, while effective for many, the limitations contained within all programs, carry with them severe long-term negative consequences for others—chief of which is pronounced reading failure.

I guess what bothers me the most is what I see as the complete lack of candor on the part of our nation's researchers, authors, and publishers. I simply cannot understand why experts and authorities cannot share the downside of their recommendations and products. In other words, why can't they be forced to mention the negative consequences associated with the use of their methods, just as drug companies are forced to mention the potential problems associated with their highly successfully clinically documented drugs?

Can you imagine the impact if parents and decision makers, who have been given the responsibility of spending enormous sums of taxpayer money, were treated to commercials such as:

"While identified as an effective and proven reading method for many students nationwide…[this method]…(You can put into the blank any of the following: phonics, sight, whole language, etc.) can exhibit the following side effects such as pronounced academic failure, discipline problems, truancy, poor self-image and the loss of high paying jobs. Severe consequences can even include retention, failure to graduate and the loss of a local, state or national election. As always, please consult with a competent professional before choosing the reading approach that is right for you or your loved ones."

What a breath of fresh air. Nevertheless, I have to stop daydreaming and get back to the harsh reality that researchers don't state openly what they discuss privately:

All reading programs carry quite debilitating and long-term negative side effects for many groups of students. These side effects include pronounced reading failure, disruptive classroom behavior, retention, the development of a lifelong negative self-image, a very small chance of finishing high school on time or with a regular diploma, almost no chance of going to college and a very, very strong chance of ending up in jail.

Why Can't Researchers Be Honest

Why can't researchers in colleges and universities be honest with our lawmakers, teachers, parents and the key decision makers in our schools?

Such honesty would go a long way in preventing some of the more horrendous curriculum decisions that are occurring daily across our nation. An example is our nation spending over a billion dollars annually in training our nation's K-3 teachers on what is essentially a "one-size fits all" reading approach for all of their students. When will researchers, publishers and policy makers stop giving the appearance of a confidence that forces (or worse, politically mandates) school districts to impose one blanket reading approach for all their students? Frankly, this arrogance borders on being criminal and usually goes unpunished.

Goes unpunished? What do I mean by that? Where are the researchers of the nineties who are publicly apologizing for what their recommendations did to our nation's currently failing seventeen year olds? Did I miss their public apology to the students, parents and teachers who were forced to use their "sure fired, can't fail, research based" methods? When did they say: "I'm sorry," or "I made a mistake"?

Don't kid yourself. These researchers knew from the beginning what could happen, but their egos just got in their way. They knew they should have explained the huge difference between statistical significance (merely meaning "greater than chance") and the probability of complete total success.

Researchers know that every study has students who fail. They also know how to extrapolate their numbers to common sense statements such as, "our research indicated that while very effective for 3 out of 5 students, this approach simply did not work for at least 1 out of 5." Statements like this would allow decision makers to make real decisions. But they weren't made then and they aren't made now.

Reading Bigotry

Let's face it; the "whole language-only" advocates caused great damage to too many students in the eighties, just as the "phonics-only" advocates are currently causing great damage to too many of our students today. This reading bigotry must be recognized for what it is and stopped.

Why does this continue to happen? First, it has to do with how researchers define reading. Which as you shall soon see is not a very easy task. Second, it has to do with ignoring those three critical reading research facts I mentioned before.

I like to tell my audiences that if I took the world's twenty leading reading researchers, locked them in a room with an armed guard standing at the only exit, and I told all twenty that the only way they could leave the room is to develop a universal definition for the term "reading," they would all starve to death before they ever left the room. This is the current state of the art in the field of how to teach reading.

There are still far too many broad, non-specific definitions on what constitutes the term "reading." Yet, the experts move forward with complete confidence. For example, for years billions of dollars were consumed on the diagnosis and treatment of dyslexia.

While I have no doubt that such a condition as dyslexia probably exists, I do think it is important to note that for many decades the key definition and therefore the basis for the identification of "dyslexic students" centered on a definition of exclusion. In other words, while the experts couldn't tell you what dyslexia was, they could tell you what it wasn't!

Dyslexia was once defined as, "a disorder manifested by difficulty in learning to read despite conventional instruction, adequate intelligence and socio-cultural opportunity," (World Federation of Neurology). What did they mean by "conventional instruction" or "adequate intelligence" or "socio-cultural opportunity"? How could you prove that conventional instruction occurred or that the student had adequate intelligence? This definition was just too broad to be useful and yet, it was used for years. This definition was the standard.

Let me make my point once again. I'm not here to repudiate the field of dyslexia. I am simply using this as an example of why we need a wake up call for policy and decision makers. The notion of "buyer beware" couldn't be more appropriate. There is a huge difference between what is presented as "hard core" research and the reality of that research. This research is namely a slowly growing, constantly evolving, highly elusive body of slightly tainted evidence.

In summary, we need to understand that the field of reading research is quite broad and the results produced by most reading programs while good, are not great. Even more important, we have to look at how these programs fit in terms of the unique needs of the learner. There is a huge difference in the terms: poor, struggling and non-readers. No one reading program can be all things to all students. This is especially true for the needs of non-readers. Make no mistake about it. Non-readers' needs are real. They do carry unique characteristics, as the next chapter will illustrate. It's up to all of us to recognize these facts in our quest to become knowledgeable consumers. Too many lives are depending on us.

Letter From a Parent...

Winston Salem, NC
June 8, 2006

I am a parent of a child that participated in the Failure Free Tutoring Program. My husband and I are very pleased with the progress that our daughter has shown since beginning this program. My daughter was a child that would just give up when she got frustrated because she couldn't do something. Reading was a really big problem for her.

The teachers that she had did not know how to reach her academically. One teacher told us that we needed to start looking at putting her in a special school because she was slow and would never be able to keep up with the other kids in the class. We had her tested and everything was normal. So we kept working with her at home, our neighbor is an instructor at the local technical institute; she tutored her on the weekends. My husband and I didn't know what else to do, then we heard about a well known tutoring institute*, we enrolled her into that program hoping that for the amount of money and time that they were charging us, we would see some kind of progress. She was there for almost a year and there was very little progress.

She got to the place that she hated to go to her tutoring sessions, it was like a chore, and we had to make her go. Her elementary school had a tutoring fair. The parents of the children that qualified had a first choice and a second choice. Failure Free was highly recommended to me by someone that knew my daughter's situation that was the first step to putting my daughter on the path to being a successful reader. Her whole outlook has changed after being in the Failure Free Reading Program. Academically she is a totally different child.

She looks forward to going to tutoring; she loves to read now and is not afraid to read out loud. Her reading level has come up from a 2nd grade level to a 6th grade level in the short time that she has been in the Failure Free Program. The instructors keep me informed of her progress. They are so excited about the children learning and making progress and that makes the kids excited and want to learn. After all that we have gone through we finally found a winner. We highly recommend this program to any and everyone.

All schools should have this program.

*name of institute was taken out of letter

(Note: The Failure Free Program is such a wonderful learning experience during the school year. Do you think it would be possible to continue the reading program during the summer? We will continue telling everyone about this wonderful program because we have proof that it really works. Thanks and keep up the good work.)

Sincerely,
John & LaTanya

Chapter 3

Three Characteristics of Non-Readers

Are there characteristics that set non-readers and very lowest literacy students apart from their achieving peers? The answer is an unequivocal yes!

My research and experience has led me to identify three characteristics that set these non-achieving students apart from their achieving peers. I call them PD, ED and LD. Please note that ED does not stand for emotionally disturbed and LD does not stand for Learning Disabled. However, let us first get a key definition out of the way before I discuss each characteristic.

What is Reading?

What do we mean by reading? No, even more realistically, what do I think the word "reading" means?

I believe that reading is gaining meaning from the printed page. No meaning equals: no reading. I believe that the reader must be able to understand the message of the writer. More importantly, I do not subscribe to the notion that reading is merely recognizing words. Why not? Too many students can be taught to read words without gaining any meaning.

More Than Word Attack

Reading is more than just recognizing words. It is a cognitive process involving the reader and the printed page. This interplay must occur between the reader and the printed page if reading for meaning is to occur.

Too often, reading is confused with successfully reading words aloud either in isolation or context. This is wrong. Reading is more than word attack or word recognition. Merely being able to figure out a word or recognizing words instantly does not insure reading success. Hard to believe? Consider the next two examples.

In the first example, I'll show you why reading is more than word attack. In a minute, I'll ask you to go to Figure 1. I want you to read the passage in Figure 1. I want you to concentrate on reading smoothly, with good cadence and expression.

However, keep this in mind: We always start from the upper right hand corner of the page and we always read from right to left! That's correct: right to left. So "hguohtla" is the word: "although."

In addition, I want you to put a little pressure on yourself. Try to read this entire passage in less than three minutes. Are you ready? Get out your timer. Turn to Figure 1. Ready, set, begin!

Figure 1:

gnileefnu dna errazib rehtar mees yam ti hguohtlA
toidi na teem ot kcul doog saw ti deveileb elpoep ,
nemrehsiF .ksat tnatropmi emos no nehw
enoyna fo htap eht ssorc ot taht dleh ralucitrap ni
rieht ot gniog nehw decnalabnu yllatnem saw ohw
lufsseccus dna efas a erusne dluow staob
taht si noititsrepus siht fo nigiro ehT .egayov
etipsed dna "roop s'doG" era elpeop hcus lla
.yaw nwo rieht ni desselb era snoitatimil rieht

Are you done? How did you do? Were you able to figure out the words? Did you read quickly, smoothly and with expression? I bet you didn't. If you're like most of us, you probably found yourself laboring painstakingly over each word as you tried to figure each word out. What about speed? Did you finish the passage in three minutes? Of course not. Did you read fluently? Or did you find yourself going word by word and letter by letter?

More importantly, was there any meaning? Did you understand what you just read aloud, even though you were able to figure out each word? I bet you didn't.

Decoding Versus Recoding

I believe that if I asked educators what the previous activity demonstrated, 99.9% of them would respond that this was a "decoding activity." They would state I was expecting them to break the code by sounding out the words. And I would respond that they were wrong. This was not a decoding activity.

OK. So why wasn't it decoding? It wasn't decoding because by its very implication, decoding means breaking the code. Breaking the code means converting the visual symbols (the letters in the words) into meaning. Did this actually happen? Were you able to understand this passage while you read it aloud? Did it make any sense after you read it? I'll bet not.

So, what did you just do? I believe that you just spent your time involved in "recoding." Recoding? Yes, recoding. Recoding is a process in which you convert one symbol system to another symbol system with the absence of meaning. Confused? Don't be.

You simply took what you saw (the visual letters and words) and gave them their name (what the letters and words sounded like) WITHOUT (and this is the key point) giving them meaning. In other words, you never broke the code because you never understood what you were saying. You were essentially "word calling" or what neuropsychologists identify as "Hyperlexia."

Developmental Hyperlexia, as I mentioned earlier in the book, is a condition that generally occurs before the age of six. Sadly, many who suffer from developmental hyperlexia are cognitively limited or have suffered from neonatal or early childhood brain injury. Parents of Developmental Hyperlexics swear that they never attempted to teach their children how to read. "They just started to read aloud," the parents would state. And read aloud they did.

Developmental Hyperlexics can read any word they see. Grade level is not an issue. Many identify words many, many years above their actual age. They can also say these words aloud whether presented to them upside down or sideways.

Developmental Hyperlexics also read without any comprehension and fluency. Usually they read in a monotone voice, don't pause for commas or stop at periods. When they are finished recoding (see how much you are learning) and are asked what they just read, they'll look you dead in the eye and say, "I don't know," and they really don't.

Let me take this issue of Hyperlexia one step further, especially as it pertains to non-brain injured and non-cognitively limited non-readers. It is my opinion that current instructional practices are actually creating a condition that I call "Acquired Hyperlexia."

An Unwanted Byproduct of Phonics Instruction

Acquired Hyperlexics mirror the behavior of Developmental Hyperlexics. The difference centers on when and how this condition occurs. Acquired Hyperlexia occurs during school age and is produced in the classroom. I believe it is an unwanted byproduct of too much emphasis on teaching phonics and word attack skills.

Unfortunately, too many students today are being taught that reading is simply getting the words correct. Their goal appears to be word-perfect reading, and in doing so, they learn to become avid recoders.

Let me get this straight. Are you saying that we are actually teaching large numbers of students to recode?

Absolutely!!! As the following example illustrates.

Who do you think makes more oral reading errors, good readers or poor readers? The answer will surprise you. Studies have shown that as a group there is no difference in the number of errors made. Good readers make just as many substitutions and omissions when they read a passage as poor readers. However, there is a difference between good and poor readers.

The difference is based on the kind of errors made. Good readers do not make haphazard guesses. They seem to understand fully that reading means gaining meaning from the printed page. Good readers therefore make meaning based errors. If they make mistakes, they will err on the side of meaning. In other words, good readers make good errors.

Consider the following sentence: "The boys and girls were playing in the yard." Suppose a student, attempting to read this sentence, said: "The kids were outside playing." What type of error did he/she make? Was it a good or a poor error?

I believe it was a good error because the student was able to show a grasp of the author's meaning. Although, it wasn't an exact match in words, it was a close match in meaning. The student demonstrated that he did comprehend even though his expressive output (the words he said aloud) did not exactly match the words on page.

Many times, poor readers are taught to make poor text-driven errors. Too often, students are taught by their teacher to ignore meaning in the quest for "decoding perfection." In doing so, teachers will actually force their students to concentrate exclusively on the print and ignore the meaning. (Remember what you did in our "right to left" reading example.)

For example, students who responded, "The kids were outside playing," would not be rewarded. Most would be told they were incorrect and to go back and first look at the letters. What are the sounds that go with the letters? Look at the beginning sounds. Look at the vowels. What sounds do they make? What are our rules about these letters and the sounds? Soon, the students only make phonetically correct errors such as, "The bays and grils were outslide paying in the year." While we can figure out how they were able to come up with what they did (concentrating too much on the letters and sounds) their response makes absolutely no sense.

PD Students

While the danger of Acquired Hyperlexia is real and is a much overlooked, there is an even greater danger associated with teaching phonics to many non-readers. It has to do with the first characteristic associated with non-readers—PD students.

PD stands for the phrase "phonetically deaf." What do you mean??? Are you telling me that phonics is bad?? I thought phonics was the answer to all of our reading woes. Isn't that what their research says? Isn't the lack of phonics a primary factor in the current mess we are in? Well, before I answer that, let me remind you about what I first said about the three key reading research facts. Remember those facts? All reading programs work; so no, I'm not saying phonics is bad. But, it's not for all students (and yes, I am saying phonics is not appropriate for many). I am not here to attack phonics. Instead, I am going to put it in its proper perspective.

Here is the plain truth. There are some students (adults as well) who will never learn to read by using phonics. They were born with a "tin ear" for sounds. Like it or not, you could dedicate the next 120 years of your professional life trying to teach letter sounds and at the end of this time, they still wouldn't get it. I know this first hand, because I am "phonetically deaf."

The Plight of the Phonetically Deaf

Let me make one key point here. I am not deaf. I hear great. I don't have a sensory impairment. I do not suffer from any hearing loss. I can pass any hearing acuity test. I just don't make sense out of many letter sounds. I have a perceptual impairment. I don't know why. Frankly, I don't care. It's not a big deal. I'm a very poor speller. That's why I have spell checker. I can recognize a misspelled word by appearance and I can use a dictionary better than most. Let me elaborate.

I barely manage to get by in the world of letter sounds and there are times when this condition really rears its ugly head. Let me give you an example of how my inability to discriminate certain letter blends disrupts my life.

I have two good friends. One is named Craig and the other Greg. I have known them for decades and yet, I am constantly calling Craig, Greg and Greg, Craig. It drives my wife crazy.

"Why do you do this?" my wife asks.

"I just can't make the distinction," I reply. And I can't. In fact, I have to mentally visualize their names and associate them with key words to make the oral distinction. I simply don't hear the distinction. Believe me; I've tried to hear the distinction over the past two decades!

In other words, I have to see in my mind the "Cr" in Craig and associate it with the "Cr" I see in the word creek. Then I have to say both words aloud in order to distinguish between Craig and Greg. Craig is the word I see that starts with the "cr" in creek. This is a lot of work. It's not easy.

My reading comprehension scores are high. I have a Doctorate in Education, written close to a dozen published journal articles, developed a complete reading intervention series, and authored dozens of student booklets and this book as well.

The Generational Lottery

I didn't need phonics to learn to read. So, don't cry for me. I was lucky. I was a winner in Reading's Generational Lottery. I was born when "sight," visual or in more common terms—"Dick and Jane" was in and phonics was out. Quite frankly, this saved my life. But you sure can cry for the millions of school age PD students who are being brutalized daily by this generation's dogmatic "phonics only" approach. These Phonetically Deaf students are failing miserably. These PD students are beating themselves up internally. They think they're at fault. They need help now.

"How can you say this?" you might ask me. Who gives me the right to attack phonics like that? How can I stand there and defy the abundant amount of research supporting phonemic awareness, phonics and phonics based remedial intervention? Didn't I read the National Reading Panel Report? Haven't I read the literature written by the experts?

Yes, I did read the report and the articles. In fact, this is one of the main reasons why I feel fully confident in taking my stance. Frankly, I only wish key decision makers had read the research as well. If they did, they might be amazed at the number of times terms such as "treatment resisters" and "non-responders" are included in almost every review of the literature.

Researchers over the past two decades have recognized students with a core deficit in phonological processes and it is no small number. Researchers, Stephanie Al Otaiba of Florida State University and Douglas Fuchs of Vanderbilt University wrote in their article, *Characteristics of Children Who Are Unresponsive to Early Literacy Intervention: A Review of the Literature* (2002), that up to 30% of regular education and 50% of special education students fail when phonics are used! These students have difficulty processing letter sounds. This group currently makes up the largest number of at-risk and severely reading disabled students. While there is no controversy that PD students exist, there is considerable disagreement over how to treat them.

Two Schools of Thought

Basically, there are two schools of thought: remedial or compensatory.

Remedial proponents attempt to eliminate phonological deficits by intensive intervention. Remedial proponents believe that students must identify and apply the relationship between sounds and letters if they are ever going to learn to read. Remedial proponents cannot fathom a world in which students can learn to read without first learning sounds. Their primary goal is to remediate this deficit. Their primary argument for teaching sounds is that there are only 44 English sounds represented by 26 letters.

Remedial proponents believe that it is impossible to memorize the millions of words contained in the English language. To them, phonic rules provide a systematic method to decode practically every word they will contact. To these proponents, learning the phonic rules provides the most logical approach to attack unknown words.

Remediation is currently the prevalent educational approach used in our schools today. Billions of dollars are being spent on remedial methods and materials designed to correct phonological deficits. Remedial proponents cite as evidence the most recent research published by the National Reading Panel and the National Research Council.

Now hold on just a minute! Didn't you just cite the very same research as the basis for your argument against remediation? Are you losing your mind? What gives?

Well, yes. You are correct. Let me explain. The systematic teaching of phonics and phonemic awareness (a fancy name for the 44 different sounds) is the heart and soul of 40% of the current federal mandate of scientifically validated reading research programs. Schools are being mandated to include training in phonemic awareness and systematic phonics in addition to vocabulary, fluency and comprehension. However, there is a problem with the remedial model; it just doesn't work for everyone!

Students Who Defy Intensive Phonic Remediation

As I mentioned, there is a significant number of students who defy intensive phonological and phonetic remediation. Like me, they have a dysfunctional "letter to sound" route. The most recent research by the National Reading Panel confirms this. The effects of phonics and phonological awareness (PA) training appears to have little impact past K—1st grade! 67% of the PA and Phonics effectiveness studies showed no meaningful improvement in Oral Reading (effect size < .3). Even worse, phonics instruction had no impact on the reading performance of low-achieving readers in grades 2-6 (effect size = .15). Systematic phonics did not improve spelling in grades 2-6 (effect size = .009) and had no impact on passage comprehension in grades 2-6 (effect size = .12).

In addition, the National Reading Panel found that one out of every six studies measuring the efficacy of systematic phonics instruction (how good it works) actually produced negative results in reading comprehension. Finally, it appears that there is a 20-hour incubation period for phonic effectiveness. More instructional time does not improve the phonemic awareness of "phonetically deaf" students. They simply do not improve much, even if they receive hundreds and hundreds of hours of more phonics.

The notion of students who can't hear sounds and subsequently cannot learn to read using phonics is not new. Special educators have been familiar with this idea for decades as demonstrated in the work of Helmer K. Myklebust in the sixties. Mykelbust, noted researcher, author, and head of the Institute for Language Disorders at Northwestern University, listed in his research classic, *Learning Disabilities Educational Principles and Practices* (1967), the following characteristics of students with what he called auditory dyslexia:

Inability to relate letters to sounds
Can't "hear" similarities in initial and final sounds ~ in words

Short vowels one of their greatest difficulties
Can recognize "pin" "pen" in context but not in ~ isolation
Can't recognize a rhyme or think of words that ~ rhyme
Can't break words into individual syllables or sounds
Can't combine the sounds to form a whole word
Can't learn to read by a phonic or elemental approach

Why can't they learn to read using a phonetic approach? Because they are, what I have already called, "phonetically deaf." "Phonetically deaf" students don't hear the sounds or can't comprehend the relationship to sounds and letters regardless of age or length of treatment. In other words, phonics "ain't ever gonna be their thing."

Therefore, the bad news is that there are large numbers of students who will not learn to read using phonics. Dr. Joe Torgeson of Florida State University, cited in, *Preventing Reading Difficulties in Young Children*, calls this group "treatment resisters." "Up to 25% of at-risk children who receive training in phonological awareness, 'gain little insight in the structure of spoken words, much less into reading by the end of training' (Torgesen et al., 1997)." Dr. Torgeson concluded by stating that another reading alternative is needed.

As I previously mentioned, Otaiba and Fuchs (2004), fully agree with Torgeson when they state, "…few researchers have suggested that either phonological awareness training or beginning decoding instruction is a silver-bullet solution that prevents reading difficulties in all children. Indeed, investigators have reported that as many as 30% of children who are at-risk for reading difficulties and as many as 50% of children who have special needs may not benefit from generally effective phonological and decoding instruction." (Page 1). They cite twenty-three different phonological and decoding intervention studies that document the existence of significant numbers of "treatment resisters" in each study.

The Good News

However, there is good news. Whether they are called "Treatment Resisters" or "Phonetically Deaf," these students can learn to read utilizing compensatory methods such as Failure Free Reading. In most cases, they can have an immediate and successful reading experience.

Compensatory proponents believe in teaching to the students' strengths. For example, the obvious alternative to help a student with poor phonics would be a "sight based" reading approach. While researchers like to get real fancy and call this an orthographic reading approach, it is still sight based. Regardless of what you call it, there appears to be very solid, credible evidence supporting a viable "sight based" reading alternative for "phonetically deaf" students. My personal experience in learning to read using the old "Dick and Jane" system confirms this.

I saw "Dick" and "Jane" repeatedly in print. I said "Dick," I said "Jane." I didn't sound out "D-i-ck" or "J-ane." I simply said, "Dick," "Jane," and "Spot." To me this was easy, I would look and then I would say! Due to this "look-say" approach, I was at the top of my class. I read Dick and Jane fluently with full comprehension. It taught to my visual strength.

Unfortunately, had I been born within the last ten years and entered one of today's phonological awareness or decoding based reading programs, I would have been at the bottom of my class with an all expenses paid ticket to special education. As I said before, I won the generational reading lottery. Dick and Jane tapped my visual strength. I was a winner, like 70% of my fellow students. "Look-say" was the current research based approach at the time I went to school. It made sense then and contrary to public opinion, "look-say" still makes sense today.

Neuro-cognitive Psychology

The "dual route theory" of oral reading supports this notion of "sight based" strength. The dual route theory is supported by data from acquired phonological and acquired surface alexic patients. In other words, neurocognitive researchers looked at patients who lost the ability to read due to a brain injury. They observed different types of reading difficulties based on where the injury occurred in the brain. These researchers called one type of reading difficulty: acquired phonological alexia, and the other acquired surface alexia.

Noted neurocognitive psychologists, Nancy Ewald Jackson and Max Colheart, mention in their book, *Routes to Reading Success and Failure* (2001), that patients with acquired phonological alexia "...have an intact 'sight word' route." It is their strength. Jackson and Colheart further state that students with acquired phonological alexia have "good reading of words with impaired reading of pseudo words." In other words, meaning is their thing. Acquired phonological alexics can easily read words like "house," "ambulance," "like," and "cat," but are totally unable to sound "phonetically regular" non-words like: "ket," "gon," or "wike."

The research pertaining to my Failure Free Reading Methodology also supports this notion of a compensatory process. Phonetically Deaf students who are born with a "tin ear" for sounds can have successful, age-appropriate reading experiences if they are allowed to use their strengths and certain variables are controlled for within the text and within the instructional procedure. What these instructional variables are exactly will be discussed later. For now, it's important to know that The Failure Free Reading Methodology is the first compensatory reading program to control for all of these variables for the "Phonetically Deaf."

The Plight of the ED Student (Environmentally Denied)

What if you didn't have to figure out any words. What if you knew every word instantly by sight? Would this be enough to guarantee success and comprehension? More importantly, would real reading for meaning take place? Maybe, maybe not. Much of this depends on whether you are ED or not. ED stands for "environmentally denied."

I believe that economics does play a key role in reading comprehension. Poor kids are not going to comprehend as well as richer kids.

What! Are you kidding?! Are you saying that poorer kids are less capable of comprehending? Are you saying that rich kids coming from upper income homes with more discretionary capital are brighter or more capable than are poor students?

No, I'm not. However, it would be naive to ignore the opportunities that abound in upper income homes. These opportunities do have an impact on reading comprehension.

For example, I am the father of five middle- to upper-income children. All five of my children are products of public schools—elementary, middle and high school. Even better, all five of my children attended Title I schools. Title I is federal aid earmarked to schools with a large concentration of students who qualify for "free or reduced" lunch. In other words, all of my five middle-upper income children shared daily classroom space with large numbers of lower income students.

"Low income" students live in poverty. They come from a home in which there is very little discretionary money available for any kind of extras. No traveling on vacations. No rides to the park. No nothing. Because of this, low-income students cannot easily relate to many story themes or topics—especially the ones most beginning reading authors think every student should know, as the following story illustrates.

A Conversation I'll Never Forget

I'll never forget a conversation I had with a southeastern elementary school building principal. His building housed a great number of "have-not," low-income students. He was a hard working, creative principal always looking for ways to improve the lives and performance of his lowest income students. I could tell the look of skepticism on his face, after I explained my "environmentally denied" theory. This skepticism became even more obvious when I ended with the notion that too often, authors of reading textbooks assume most students can easily relate to their story's theme. This principal, like most of his colleagues, believed this as well.

A short time later, I received a call from this principal. He was calling to apologize about his skepticism toward my "assume too much" comment. I asked what caused his change of heart. He said it was what he had witnessed last weekend. As I mentioned, this was an innovative principal. He thought out of the instructional box. One of his pet projects was his "hands on" science class for his fifth graders. As an end of the year reward, all fifth graders went on a weekend trip to the coast to do an environmental study. The coast was four hours away.

The principal reminded me that he had been principal in this building for over eight years. He prided himself on knowing all his students. He knew many of his fifth graders since they attended his preschool program. He thought he knew everything about his fifth graders and yet...

He said everything went well on the trip to the beach. They had a great bus trip and arrived early. As a treat, he thought he would take them to the beach and let them play in the ocean. No big deal.

However, it was a very big deal. The principal said he was amazed when he saw the look of astonishment and surprise on the majority of his fifth graders' faces. Rather than run, they just stopped, stood and stared in amazement. It took the principal a few moments to realize what was happening. This moment was a huge eye opener for him. For many of his students, this was the first time they had ever been to the beach. They never saw or heard the sounds of waves. After the initial awe wore off, they began laughing, giggling and running in and out of the water.

Then it hit him. He thought of all the years and all the stories these students, were asked to read about going to the beach or being at the seashore. How difficult this must have been for many of these students in preschool and the early grades. No wonder their comprehension scores were so poor.

After he told me his story, I replied, "You're right! Relating is the key to comprehension. How can you teach a story about cows when a majority of your students think milk comes from the refrigerator?" I asked. My point was this: there is no way we should assume that these students know the relationship between milk and cows. We should take nothing for granted. While this is true for any student, this is especially true for our Environmentally Deprived students.

Sadly, far too many low-income students are coming to school with very little educationally relevant experiences. Their parents are limited financially. Many work two jobs. Many are single parents. These parents are exhausted when they come home. They don't have the extra cash to take out their children. While they clearly want what's best for their kids, they are severely limited by their financial resources.

It is our job as teachers and educators to be absolutely certain that our students have the necessary background experiences to relate to the story we are asking them to comprehend. If they lack the appropriate background experiences, then we have to build on what they bring to the task. In other words, it is up to us to bridge the "experiential divide" as I had to do when I visited a particular western Virginia middle school.

A Trip to Virginia

I was recently asked to travel to the western part of Virginia to give a demonstration of Failure Free Reading to a school district. As is my custom, I asked to work with one of their worst students. They introduced me to an eighth grade special education student.

The boy was classified as severely learning disabled and was a virtual non-reader. He had been in special education for over three years and had shown absolutely no growth—regardless of the reading method used. The school district was at its wits end. Years of good teachers, money invested, and nationally recognized remedial reading approaches had produced an eighth grade special education student with an independent reading level of pre-primer.

As usual, when I showed the group of special educators the passage that I was about to teach, I was told, "No way, he won't be able to comprehend this. It's way too hard!" Again, I thought to myself, "Let's just see."

The school district was located in the western part of Virginia—many mountains and few people. There were few stores and certainly no large shopping malls. Why do I mention this? Because the grade level passage I was to teach this non-reader was about shopping at a downtown mall.

Building on the Base

I felt certain that this was a low-income student who had probably never been outside of his immediate area and never been to a mall. So, how was I going to bridge this instructional gap? How was I going to explain the concept of a "mall" to a student who had never directly experienced a mall? The answer was simple: "build on his base."

But what was his base? A few quick questions soon answered that. "Where does your family go to shop for non-grocery items," I asked. "Wal-Mart," he said. "Good." I thought, "now that I know your base, I'll relate Wal-Mart (something he has directly experienced) to a downtown mall," (something he currently could not comprehend).

"Imagine you were going to buy some clothes, a DVD and some shampoo at Wal-Mart," I said. "Would you find all of them in the same place?"

"No." He said, "I'd have to go to different places in the store."

"That's right," I said. "They call these different places 'departments'."
"For example, you would buy the clothes in the clothes department, the DVD in electronics department and the shampoo near the drug store department. Does this idea of 'departments' make sense to you?" I asked.

"Yes," he said.

"Now imagine that instead of Wal-Mart, we were in a large area made up of many small stores. Each store was just like a department in Wal-Mart. Each store sold something special like clothes, electronics, jewelry and so on. Imagine twenty or fifty of these stores all in one place where you can walk from store to store under one roof. Do you know what they call this?"

"No." He said.

"They call it a 'mall,' In other words, a 'mall' is just a fancy name for a place where there is a large group of stores all under one roof instead of Wal-Mart's departments all in one building. Does the word 'mall' make sense to you now?" I asked again.

"Yes." he said.

A little while later, the boy read aloud an age-appropriate passage about a trip to the downtown shopping mall. The passage was at least five grade levels higher than the boy's independent reading level. He read it fluently, with expression and full comprehension.

Why full comprehension? Because, as I said before, I assumed nothing and built on his base. I went forward only after he said he fully understood each key term or concept contained in the passage. When I was completely satisfied that he could relate to what I was about to teach, I presented the passage to him. His performance (reading aloud fluently with full comprehension) confirmed how well I taught this Environmentally Denied (ED) student. I assumed nothing and built directly upon his base. I defined each key word or concept in terms that he could easily relate.

In closing, I have an activity that I believe will demonstrate what it feels like to be Environmentally Denied. I think you will be quite amazed.

An ED Demonstration

In a moment, I want you to read the passage in Figure 2. When you are finished, jot down as many notes as you can about what you just read. Finally, give the passage a comprehensibility ranking ranging from 7 (very comprehensible) to 1 (very incomprehensible).

Figure 2:

The procedure is actually quite simple. First, you arrange things into different groups. Of course, one pile may be sufficient depending on how much there is to do. If you have to go somewhere else due to lack of facilities, that is the next step, otherwise you are pretty well set. It is important not to overdo things. That is, it is better to do too few things at once than too many. In the short run, this may not seem important, but complications can easily arise. A mistake can be expensive as well. At first, the whole procedure will seem complicated. Soon, however, it will become just another facet of life. It is difficult to foresee any end to the necessity for this task in the immediate future, but then one can never tell. After the procedure is completed, one arranges the materials into different groups again. Then they can be put in their appropriate places. Eventually they will be used once more and the whole process will have to be repeated. However, that is part of life.

—Author Unknown

How did you do? Did you have difficulty recognizing any of the words? No, I didn't think you would. What information did you gain from the passage? What did you write down? Are your notes very meaningful? Do they make sense? How did you rank the passage? Did you give it a "7" or were you like most of us and gave it a "2" or "1" or even "0"?

Why didn't this passage make sense? It certainly wasn't because you couldn't recognize every word was it? No, of course not. You recognized every word didn't you? In fact, if I were to give you a word recognition test on every word used to create this story, I'd bet that you would probably receive a score of a hundred percent. Yet, even with perfect word recognition, it didn't make any sense. Let me say again, while scoring a hundred percent in word recognition, you'd walk away with a reading comprehension score of zero!

What was missing? What caused you to stop having a successful reading for meaning experience? The fact that I prevented you from being able to relate to the story from your own personal experience stopped you from having a successful experience. You couldn't relate to it, you could not read it for meaning. Why couldn't you relate to it? Because you didn't know what the story was about.

What was missing from this passage was the key element that allows you to relate. That's right; you needed to know the title for this passage.

Without a title, you simply couldn't relate to the passage no matter how easily you recognized the words contained in it. Now go back to Figure 2 and read the passage one more time, now that you know the title of the passage is, "How to Wash Clothes."

How did you do this time? Isn't the difference in comprehension amazing? Were you surprised to see how well written and concise this seemingly rambling and meaningless passage has become? Fortunately, most successful students have the necessary background and experiences needed to relate easily to the material presented to them. Most non-readers do not. As I've already said, this is not due to a cognitive limitation. Obviously, high-income students are not any smarter than low-income.

Nurture Over Nature

I truly believe that if I could magically drop a low-income student into the world of the high-income student, the low-income student would perform as well as his high-income peer. It's all economics. In this case, nurture clearly has a decisive advantage over nature.

The high-income students weren't born smarter than low-income students. I don't believe that for one minute. It's all economics. Students who come from wealthier parents are given more opportunities and exposure to more people, places and things. Let's face it, students whose parents take them to the beach, or the mountains, or the theater, or on hikes are going to have more background experiences to draw from when reading stories about the beach, or the mountains, or the theater, or hikes.

Students whose parents are working two jobs and are barely getting by are not in a position to provide a wide variety of cultural experiences no matter how much they want to do this for their children. So high-income students only "appear" smarter because their prior experiences allow them to speak on a larger range of topics and interests. It's all about exposure.

Reading comprehension is dependent on "nurture" (where "nurture" is measured by experiential opportunities, not love). The more a student knows about a topic prior to reading it, the more the student will understand it as he reads it. Much of our Environmentally Denied students' problems are clearly dependent upon their financial "lot in life."

The LD Student

Here is an interesting statement. I believe that poor reading is not really the problem. How can I say that? Let me explain.

I believe we are spending too much time treating the symptoms and not enough time treating the disease. As far as I'm concerned, poor reading is just a symptom of a much larger problem. I'll go even further. Poor reading can be likened to a bad case of the flu where phonics is Nasal Spray, whole language is a vapor rub, and sight words are cough drops. However, Language Development is penicillin!

The real key to reading success is not found in letters and sounds, but in vocabulary. Students cannot comprehend above their language level of comprehension. In other words, no eighth grade student will ever comprehend eighth grade reading material when he/she carries a second or third grade vocabulary. The primary instructional focus of any reading intervention has to be on the development of a student's receptive language ability. Everything else pales in comparison.

Two Levels of Language

There are two levels of language. The first is the level of language understanding. The second is the level of language expression. Understanding comes first.

Receptive language is the language level of understanding. It measures what a student is able to comprehend when written material is presented orally. It is an individual's listening comprehension level. For example, let's say you read a seventh grade book aloud to a seventh grade student. The student appears to be listening. The student's look is focused and attentive.

Upon completion of the passages or story, you ask a series of questions about what you just read aloud. The student answers every question correctly. Would it be correct to state that the student has a receptive language level of at least seventh grade? I would say yes.

What if the student didn't understand what you just read aloud? Would it be fair to assume that this student is not capable of comprehending this seventh grade material? Again, I would say yes. If students can't comprehend a passage when it is presented orally, they will not comprehend it when reading silently. Improving receptive language is the starting point for improving reading comprehension.

The reasons why students can't comprehend language on grade level are many. Granted, some special education students are cognitively limited due to a developmental delay or brain injury. This is a fact of life.

Language Deprived the Third Characteristic

Fortunately, the vast majority of non-reading students are not developmentally delayed or brain injured. The vast majority of non-readers are LD. In this case, however, LD does not stand for Learning Disabled. LD stands for Language Deprived—the third key characteristic of non-readers.

Language Deprived students come to school significantly behind their achieving peers. Many come from homes in which Standard English is either not spoken or is used infrequently, as the following federal study documents.

Vocabulary—A Strong Predictor of Reading Success

In, *Start Early, Finish Strong: How to Help Every Child Become a Reader*, a publication created by the U.S. Department of Education that provides the latest research and recommendations to help all children succeed in reading, researchers mention that the size of a young child's vocabulary is a strong predictor of reading success. The National Research Council also supports this idea when they state, "Preschoolers with large vocabularies tend to become proficient readers," (1998). Finally, "To succeed at reading, children need basic vocabulary, some knowledge of the world around them, and the ability to talk about what they know…Research shows a strong connection between reading and listening" (*What Works* (1986), p15).

Many non-readers have great difficulty with the meanings of words. Researchers call this semantics. Again, I need to remind you that this difficulty is not due to a lack of cognitive ability. It is due to a lack of exposure. While just as bright as their achieving peers, non-readers fail because of the lack of exposure to the language skills necessary for reading and writing success such as vocabulary, speaking and listening. Many are born into homes where their parents either do not speak the language or are language deprived themselves.

Non-readers must not be denied access to the tools they need to read at grade level. They need to be systematically exposed to a large volume of words within meaningful contexts daily. For example, it is estimated that 3 year olds coming from higher income homes are exposed to twenty million more words than their lower income playmates. Twenty million more words! Yet we start them out in school by stressing "ah" "buh" "cuh" "duh"? I don't think so. It has to be language first and reading skills a very distant second. We can't change this order.

Language First—Reading Second

Exposure to language is critical. There is no such thing as too early to start teaching language, as the following story illustrates.

I am happily the father of five children. When I first found out that my wife, Angela, was pregnant, I started talking to my first child, Tess, when she was still in the womb. I would talk to Tess every night. I talked to her using sophisticated language; I continued this during her preschool years. We had what I called "the word for the day." Many times, I would tell Tess, as a two year old, "The word for today is 'kinesiology'." I would ask, "Tess, can you say 'kinesiology'?" Sometimes I got a garbled reply. I would then say, "Fantastic! Kinesiology means the study of movement. A Kinesiologist is someone who studies movement."

Imprinting for Future Success

Was I crazy? Did I really expect a two year old to repeat what I was saying or actually comprehend it? Of course not! I simply wanted Tess to be familiar with sophisticated language at a very young age. I was teaching to her receptive language level. I knew that the more she heard sophisticated language at an early level, the more relaxed she would be with it at a later age. I was imprinting for future success.

Tess is now a college senior at a major southeastern university with an excellent command of language, as her degree in public relations will attest. My point is it is not "illiteracy that breeds illiteracy," it's that "low language breeds low language."

Tess was very lucky. She lived in a house with parents committed to promoting, within Tess, a command of our language. Tess was fortunate.

She was living in a household where her parents took every opportunity to expose her to language.

The Federal Government did a study in which they looked at preschoolers' in-home exposure to language. The results further support the Language Deprived theory. Researchers broke the preschoolers into three groups based on their parents' economic status. One group of parents was on welfare, the second came from blue-collar homes, and the third, the homes of professionals. The differences between households were dramatic.

In this study, the professional preschool language parents exposed their children to 2100 words an hour. Blue-collar parents exposed their children to 1500 words an hour. Welfare parents exposed their children to 600 words an hour. Can you believe this? A 1500 word difference in one hour between upper and lower income students. By the time they entered school, the upper income preschoolers had been exposed to 48 million words while their lower income playmates were only exposed to 13 million. A 35 million word difference in the first four years of life!

Multi-syllable Phobic

Too many students are coming from homes where Standard English is not the spoken language. In addition, many students have parents who are "multi-syllable phobic." They are literally afraid of large words. These parents fear embarrassment and they don't want to appear foolish. Sadly, they have learned through painful experience that people will judge them the moment they open up their mouth.

What a tragedy. Individuals with 140 or higher "potential IQs," are being judged on their current 80 or 90 present IQ vocabulary! Why? Because they have never been exposed to 140 IQ words. If they weren't exposed, how can we expect their children to be exposed? I believe this is where school must come in. In most cases, formal language instruction does not even enter the picture.

The Importance of Vocabulary

Vocabulary is one of the key ingredients in reading comprehension. Again, let me say this one more time, students with larger vocabularies do better in school. We've known this for over a half a century. Smith's research published in, *Genetic Psychological Monographs* (1941), found that successful high school seniors knew four times as many words as their low performing peers and, even more dramatic, high performing third graders had a personal vocabulary greater than low performing twelfth graders. Yet, 65 years later, and the formal instruction in vocabulary has all but been ignored in the traditional classroom.

This notion that formal instruction has all but been ignored is further underscored by Natalie Rathvon, in her book, *Effective School Interventions* (1999), when she cites that, "teachers spend little time helping students learn or practice new vocabulary during reading lessons. Durkin (1978-79), found that only 19 minutes of 4,469 total minutes of reading instruction (less than 0.5%) was devoted to vocabulary instruction. Similarly, Roser and Juel (1982) mention that teachers '...spent an average of only 1.67 minutes on vocabulary during each reading lesson.'"

Can you believe it? We spend hours and hours each day on teaching students to sound words out and almost nothing on teaching what the words mean. If this doesn't illustrate the foolishness of "putting the cart before the horse," then nothing can. This certainly goes a long way in explaining why by third grade, at-risk students trained in word attack do so poorly (and actually lose ground) in reading comprehension. At-risk students need to be immersed daily in explicit vocabulary lessons. Vocabulary must be rich, real, and directly tied into their current vocabulary base. We have to build on that base.

Building on the base must always be coupled with the ultimate goal of dramatically expanding their vocabulary. The good news is that non-readers can learn to expand their vocabulary (Kuhn and Stahl, 2000). They are not "less capable." Stahl cites the "Mathew Effect" as the chief reason for poor vocabulary growth of non-readers.

The "Mathew Effects in Reading" was first introduced to reading research by noted Canadian researcher, K.E. Stanovich, in 1986. The article is based on the biblical saying "the rich get richer and poor get poorer." Good readers expand their vocabulary by reading more than poor readers. Poor readers, therefore, fall further and further behind because they are exposed to fewer and fewer new words in their limited independent reading level context. It's not a lack of ability. It's a lack of exposure. Makes sense doesn't it? If vocabulary growth is dependent upon reading new books and material, how can non-readers ever overcome this gap? Does not seem like there's any hope. Fortunately, there is hope—lots of it. The hope comes from the concept of "reading neutrality."

Reading Neutrality

For the past thirty years, I have been creating what I call "reading neutral" instructional materials for non-readers. The concept is simple. It is designed to "level the playing field" for non-readers, by giving them the opportunity to show what they are capable of doing when reading isn't an issue.

What are you saying this time? I'm saying that we can give non-readers the chance to close the vocabulary gap with their achieving peers by exposing them to large numbers of words in meaningful "reading neutral" contexts.

The key to successful "reading neutral" instruction centers on three words: oral, explicit and exposure. How do we expose non-readers to more and more print? By reading it aloud to them. Stahl mentions, "several studies have found that children can learn words as efficiently from having stories read to them as from reading stories themselves." For example, Stahl, Richek, and Vandevier (1990) found that sixth graders learned about as many word meanings from a single listening as they would learn from a single reading. This was especially true for children with vocabulary knowledge (p.13). This growth becomes even more pronounced when students are placed in "reading neutral" materials that control for the three instructional variables essential for non-reader's success. I will discuss each in the next chapter.

Teacher Testimonial...

What Failure Free Reading Has Done For My Deaf Students

For deaf students, the key to the English language is the written text. Typically deaf students struggle with vocabulary and reading comprehension. Many have lower reading levels than their hearing peers. Because deaf students never hear the spoken word, reading instruction needs to provide enough written vocabulary repetition for the students to learn and retain new vocabulary. As is true with all readers, it is imperative that teachers present age-appropriate, meaningful story content. Traditional reading programs work with some of our students, but with other students, they do not. It is often times difficult to find appropriate materials for our truly struggling readers.

With adaptations made for the deaf, *Failure Free Reading* has been successfully used with thirteen to fifteen-year old non-readers and limited readers. It provides the repetitive vocabulary and meaningful age-appropriate content that our remedial students need. These students are now motivated and want to read. They are feeling more and more confident and requiring less and less assistance. When implementing this program, most of the students were on a beginning first grade reading level. By the end of the year, they were successfully participating in a basal reader program and able to read second and some third-grade library books. That is a huge accomplishment considering that prior to using *Failure Free Reading*; these teenagers had never experienced independent, successful reading.

In addition to skills and confidence, *Failure Free Reading* has given these students pride. For the first time ever, these remedial students were proud to show the more accomplished students their vocabulary lists and reading stories. Finally, these students, too, were addressing age-appropriate vocabulary.

Toward the end of the year, some of the students began to complain that the *Failure Free Reading* lessons were boring and too repetitive. They preferred the basal readers recently introduced or library books. At first I was perplexed, but then it all made perfect sense. *Failure Free Reading* has served its purpose and has been successful! I sincerely believe that *Failure Free Reading* provided the "jump start" these students needed to join the more traditional programs and to begin enjoying the school library. What an accomplishment!

Laurie Grier—Classroom Teacher of the Deaf—Middle School

Chapter 4

Three Instructional Elements for Reading Success

One of my favorite phrases is, "if you always do what you always done, you always get what you always got!" So, what does this mean? It means that by now, the following fact should be crystal clear: "Non-readers are different." They can never succeed doing the "same old same old." They need to be placed in different instructional materials that are specifically designed to promote their success.

Unlike other reading intervention programs, Failure Free Reading is different in that it provides simultaneous access to the three instructional elements crucial for the reading success of non-readers. It is the first program to take the position that blame should not be placed on the student, parent or teacher without first looking at the appropriateness of the instructional materials and methodology.

Too often, it is assumed that non-readers are placed in instructional material that is in its simplest form. Nothing could be farther from the truth. We can't ignore the text we are using to teach. As Elfrieda H. Hiebert (1998) at the Center for the Improvement of Early Reading Achievement states, "text does matter in the teaching of reading."

So what are these three key instructional elements? They are repetition, sentence structure and story content. As you shall soon see, the ability for non-readers to access simultaneously these three critical instructional elements has never existed, until now.

Repetition

The more students can instantly recognize words, the easier reading aloud will become. So how do students instantly recognize words? How do they get to the point that they know the words well enough to read successfully aloud? The answer lies in the world of cognitive neuropsychiatry and what is called the "dual-route theory of reading."

In their book, *Routes to Reading Success and Failure*, internationally known neuropsychiatrists, Nancy Jackson and Max Coltheart, describe the processes in which the brain is able to recognize individual words. According to Jackson and Coltheart, successful word recognition is in two parts. First, students must see the text or letters that make up the words in print (called orthography) and then they must say the name of the word aloud (called phonology).

Two Processing Routes

A healthy brain utilizes two word processing routes. One route concentrates on recognizing and pronouncing the whole word. This is called the lexical route. The second route involves the relationship between letter and sounds. This is called the nonlexical route.

Why two different routes? Probably because the brain recognizes two different sets of words in the English language. One set follows predictable sound symbol patterns. These words are phonetically regular. They are the cornerstone in demonstrating the importance and usefulness of knowing the relationship between letters and letter sounds. This process is commonly known as phonemic awareness. Knowledge of just a few of the beginning letter sounds will go a long way in helping beginning readers figure out what it feels like to read aloud by sounding out words. Educators call this process "decoding." The ability to decode appears to be housed in the non-lexical route.

Decoding is quite valuable. For example, look at what can happen when a beginning reading student learns the name of the letter: "A," and the sounds representing four letter consonants: "t," "c," "p," "s" along with the short vowel "a" and one letter combination: "ur." With this knowledge, the students could easily decode and read aloud the following sentence, "A cat purrs."

In addition, this same student could now recognize words such as pat, tap, cap, caps, taps, and sap among others. Not bad for a short period of instructional time and energy. It is this broad applicability that makes the concept of phonemic awareness and the rules associated with these letters and sounds (phonics) so attractive to educators, researchers, parents, and politicians. It seems so logical. Learn the letter sound relationships and unlock tens of thousands of words. Piece of cake. Case closed. No argument. Phonics is the only way to fly. Well, not really.

Here is an interesting question: can you tell me what the words: "the" and "there" have in common? What is the answer? These words are not easily decodable. In fact, they are not decodable at all. Educators call these words exceptions.

Exceptions are words that follow no predictable sound symbol pattern. These words are phonetically irregular. Why? Because many of these words were adopted in English from the languages of other countries as millions and millions of immigrants from different nations and cultures were absorbed into the American life style. Exceptions form the words that anti-phonics advocates list as their key reasons for why phonics can't work. Processing exceptions is the job of the lexical route.

The Brain's Two Routes of Word Processing

Let's review. The non-lexical route is designed to help the brain map sounds to the letters of the alphabet. It is where phonics lives. It is here that phonetically regular words are decoded or "sounded out."

The lexical route houses the brain's ability to recognize and instantly pronounce whole words. These words are not decoded or broken down by letters and letter sound combinations. They are simply immediately identified by sight. It is how word exceptions are identified. Neuropsychologists have called the lexical route the brain's "visual" route. It is where the brain stores all of the word exceptions. The brain doesn't bother to sound these words out. It learns these words by memory and contact—lots of it!

The Importance of Repetition

Repetition is critical to the learning process of non-readers who are phonetically deaf. They crave it. It is a "must have" for their educational survival.

Too often, repetition has a bad reputation within educational circles. Educators have become so preoccupied with the negative side of "drill and kill" that they forget the need for pronounced contact with words for the beginning reader—regardless of age. This need for repetition is especially important for our severely failing students. For these non-readers, repetition is not boring; it is the "mother of learning!"

Beginning reading students learn to recognize words at considerably different contact rates. The average beginning reading student, regardless of age, needs to see a word somewhere between 25 to 45 times before they can recognize most sight words without any assistance. Some students need as much as three or four or more times this amount in order to instantly recognize the very same words. This is especially true for non-readers. All too often, they fail to get the required amount of repetition they need to independently recognize sight words from traditional reading materials.

Sight words? Sadly, as I have already mentioned, some words are not phonically regular. These words violate the alphabetic principle. For example, noted author and professor at the University of Tennessee, Knoxville, Charles H. Hargis, states that "more than 20 percent of first-grade level high-frequency words are not decodable by phonic analysis" (2000, p 523).

High frequency means words that are used quite often. Edwin Dolch of the University of Chicago did research in the fifties and early sixties about the frequency of words in the English language. It is classic research. His results, which have stood the test of time, might surprise you.

Dolch found that English is a very redundant language. How redundant? Well consider this: Dolch listed 220 of the most redundant words in the English language. These words (commonly referred to as the "Dolch 220") were called high frequency because they accounted for over 55% of the words students will contact between the first and ninth grade.

Can you imagine? Learn these 220 words and your students (or child) will recognize almost 1 out of every 2 words they will encounter in their first nine grades of schooling.

Multiple Exposures

Jean McCormick, former professor at Ohio State University, wrote in 1994 that while repetition is a supportive condition in word learning for most students, it is the degree of repetition that is of concern for non-readers. It appears that non-readers need significantly more contact to produce mastery or what National Reading Panel member, Dr. Jay Samuels, calls "automaticity."

Automaticity is a term that has been driving word recognition instruction since Samuels first coined it in 1974. What Samuels said is quite simple and quite important. According to Samuels, the brain is limited in the amount of cognitive energy or brainpower it can use at any one time. The brain is a single channel processor. Which means, try as you might, the brain can only think about one thing at a time. In other words, the brain cannot simultaneously process two different thoughts at the exact same moment in time. It is a physical impossibility.

Now wait a minute you might ask? Are you saying that you cannot do two or more different things at once? Why I can drive a car and talk on the cell or work in the kitchen and talk with my friends. In other words, my daily life is filled with multitasking. How does this reconcile with the brain's inability to process multiple tasks simultaneously? This is where the notion of automaticity comes into play. Automaticity or over-learning allows us to multitask.

Automaticity is the brain's answer to energy conservation. Automaticity is based on the notion of over-learning. In other words, we have learned a task so well and done it so often (repetition) that it now becomes automatic. We no longer have to think about it. It moves from the conscious to the unconscious level. It just occurs. Given this, we are now free to give our conscious attention to something new and different.

So how does the notion of automaticity tie into the teaching of reading? If the brain uses all of its conscious energy to figure out the name of strange words, it will have little energy left to recognize what that word means as the following illustrates.

Decoding means breaking the code. Taking the print that is in front of the eyes and giving it meaning. Proponents of decoding believe that quick automatic decoding skills are the key to future comprehension. They believe that once students reach the point where they can instantly decode words, it will free the brain to concentrate exclusively on what these words mean. In most cases, this is exactly what happens. Sometimes this system goes wrong, terribly wrong.

It is not unusual for teachers or parents to complain or become alarmed when they watch their students or children read aloud. Many students will read the words in the passage aloud with one hundred percent accuracy. Yet, when you ask them what they just read, they will look you straight in the eye and say: "I don't know!" They are not kidding; they really do not know what they just read!

Never Comprehended a Single Word

Why? Because they never read. What? That's right, they never comprehended a single word even though they were able to get all of the words correct! Then, what did they do if they did not decode the words on the page? Simple. You guessed it, they merely "recoded."

Recoding, as I've mentioned before, means merely swapping one code or symbol system (the actual print on the page) with another code or symbol system (the name that goes with the print). Too often, poor readers believe that reading is simply saying the words aloud and getting their names right. All of their available brainpower goes to the successful completion of this word recognition task.

But why no comprehension? Because the students are using all of their available brainpower to process the words and not the passage. In fact, the student probably does not even recognize a passage. All he or she sees is the individual words on the page in no particular order nor within any meaningful context. The student merely sees words to be "sounded out" as you and I would see random words on a vertical list. For example, consider the following sentence:

"The man waited patiently in the airport."

While you and I recognize the words as words in a sentence moving left to right, horizontally across the page and "held together by meaning," students who are stuck at the "recoding" stage might actually fail to see any relationship at all. They could actually view them as totally unrelated words—very similar to those contained in a vertical list such as:

The
waited
man
patiently
in
airport
the

Perhaps this explains why these students don't stop at commas or pause at periods, because these students are not reading for meaning. There is no importance for commas and periods. A closer examination of how they read confirms this. These students are merely saying words aloud (recoding) with little or no expression. Moreover, when they are done, they do not have a clue as to the meaning the writer tried to convey. They have exhausted all of their conscious, cognitive energy in sounding out words. These students need a viable, instructional, non-phonic alternative in order to succeed. Fortunately, this alternative can be found in one word: repetition.

The Need for Repetition

Non-readers need pronounced practice or contact with words. This is especially true for students stuck at recoding. Hargis (1992) states, "that the amount of repetition required for a student [...with reading difficulties...] to learn to recognize a word was very closely related to how much reading skill he or she had already acquired." In Hargis' study, third grade students with severe reading difficulties needed a minimum of 76.12 repetitions in order to recognize words automatically (compared to 34.5 repetitions for those reading at the third grade level) this rule held true, regardless of chronological age and IQ. It appears that non-readers need significantly more contact to produce mastery or what Samuels (1988) called "automaticity." This is further illustrated by the following formula developed by Jean McCormick (1994):

Successful Reading Instruction = ME + MC

McCormick conducted an exhaustive review on how popular reading strategies work for non-readers. She concluded by stating that most of the most well known reading intervention programs had little impact on non-readers, often after years of intensive one on one instructional practices. However, there was a glimmer of hope.

McCormick said of the programs that showed at least some promise, they were programs that stressed "ME + MC." ME stands for Multiple Exposures. MC represents Multiple Contexts. In other words, non-readers must have repeated exposure to print material within many different instructional contexts.

So there you have it. The first instructional element crucial for non-readers is repetition. Non-readers need an enormous amount of repetition. So why aren't they getting this abundance of contact? There are at least three reasons preventing the abundant use of repetition in the classroom.

First, because it is too darn hard to teach. In fact, from a teacher's perspective, it's down right boring. They do not want to hear the same words in the same sentences in the same stories over and over again. As I tell teachers across the nation, "I'm not here for you, I'm here for your non-readers!" For non-readers, repetition within a meaningful context is the key to success.

Second, as I previously mentioned, the need for repetition is often confused with the outdated and very tedious concept of "drill and kill." Critics correctly cited that, aside from the obvious problems associated with boredom, such a procedure did not lead to word generalizations. The students knew the words only on the flash cards but did not recognize them in context. There appeared to be very little transfer of learning. This is why a meaningful context is so important.

Third, most publishers are ignoring the importance of repetition within their instructional stories and materials. Word recognition is being ignored even though Juel and Roper-Schneider (1985) reported that the number of word repetitions in a story predicted how well the student would read that story. Elfrieda H. Hiebert (1998) at the Federally funded Center for the Improvement of Early Reading Achievement (CIERA) (a collaborative center, housed at the University of Michigan and dedicated to improving children's reading achievement through research-based, practical solutions to persistent problems in the learning and teaching of beginning reading), examined the types of books and stories available to beginning readers. Hiebert found that many beginning reading materials put students in stories that introduced them to too many unique words (new words) per story and presented these new words with very little redundancy. For example, a story might introduce a new word once and never use the word again in the same story.

Word Density Ratio

Hiebert described word repetition in a story through word-density ratio. She found that the average word density ratio of unique words to the total words in the story in literature-based reading programs was 1:4 and 1:2 in little book programs. In other words, beginning readers were being introduced to new words at an average rate of one new word for every four words in one reading series and as high as one new word for every two words in another series. This is simply too much too soon for too many students, regardless of age. The importance of repetition and practice for non-readers is clearly being overlooked.

The Importance of Sentence Structure

Did you know that how you write something is almost as important as what you are trying to communicate? Linguists (those who study the structure of our language) talk about the distinction between "surface structure" and "deep meaning." Surface structure is the way in which a story is written. It is the writer's use of grammar. Not all stories are written equally from a grammatical point of view.

Certain sentence structures are harder to understand than are others. The most basic sentence structure is called a "kernel sentence." Kernel sentences are characterized by the fact that they are simple, positive, active and declarative. Sentences that change anyone of these characteristics become more difficult to understand, and are therefore much more complex.

Syntactically Challenged

Sentence structure directly influences comprehension. Most students intuitively learn the basic rules of grammar at home. Unfortunately, many non-readers are limited in their knowledge of these rules. They are coming from homes in which Standard English is not the spoken language and because of this, they become "syntactically challenged." They cannot deal with complex grammatical sentence structures because they are not familiar with them.

Consider the following sentences, "The boy rode the horse." "The horse was ridden by the boy." Although both sentences mean the same thing, the first is much easier to read and understand because of the sentence structure. The first sentence is an active sentence. Notice how the boy rode the horse, flows in a natural progression; "The boy" performed an action in a logical sequence. The boy "rode." What did he ride? The boy rode "the horse." The boy was actively engaged in the act of riding. This is a simple, active, declarative sentence. This is the most basic grammatical unit of comprehension.

The second sentence is a passive sentence. The sentence does not follow a natural order of progression. Passive sentences change the logical order of progression and add a prepositional phrase. They are also written in the past tense. This causes the sentence to contain more words that are written in a more awkward fashion. "The horse," which is now presented first (out of logical sequence) was ridden (passive sentence) by the boy (prepositional phrase). In order to comprehend this, the student must perform mental gymnastics and actually rearrange the order and change the tense in his/her mind. As you can see, authors who chose complex sentence structures make their stories much harder to understand (deep meaning).

Sentence structure is the most overlooked area in the teaching of reading. In most cases, sentence structure is not even considered by authors or publishers. This is especially true when it comes to the use of readability formulas to measure the complexity of beginning reading stories.

Readability Formulas

Readability formulas are used to determine the grade level of reading material. Readability formulas are based on the number of words in a sentence and the number of syllables in a word.

It is believed that longer sentences containing larger numbers of multi-syllable words are more difficult to read. This is generally true as long as they remain predictable sentences. Sometimes, however, sentences are artificially manipulated to make a story conform to a lower readability formula. When this occurs, however, the story actually becomes more difficult to read because the sentences actually become more awkward and grammatically complex.

High Interest—Low Readability

Non-readers often have great difficulty reading material identified as high interest—low readability. Why? Because of the difference between the terms "readability" and "comprehensibility."

Let me illustrate the difference between the terms "readability" and "comprehensibility." As a former special education director, I purchased quite a bit of high interest-low readability material. I was intrigued by the opportunity to purchase material that was age-appropriate in subject matter, yet written at a level low enough for my very low-level readers. I figured it was a good purchase: interesting content for middle or high school students reading at a second grade level or below. Was I right? Not quite.

I found that while the material worked quite well for students with moderate and mild reading difficulties (those who could read somewhat), it had little effect or no effect on my most severe non-readers (those who couldn't read at all!). I was very disappointed. I bought high interest—low readability materials mainly because of my non-readers. Non-readers were the group I most wanted to help. I always wondered why high-interest low readability materials didn't work for non-readers. Now, I finally know why.

The Ten-Word Chop

The answer to why the high interest-low readability stories failed for my non-readers had to do with what I now call "the ten-word chop." Let me explain. Imagine you are asked to write a high interest story for non-reading adolescents. You must make it something they will really enjoy. You must write about a topic in which they are interested. Therefore, you decide to write a story on a subject very near and dear to an adolescent's heart, something that will hold their attention. You found the topic. You are going to write about teenage dating. Who could argue that a story on teenage dating wouldn't be of high interest to adolescent non-readers? When you finish your manuscript, you send it off to the publisher.

The publisher receives your manuscript and immediately sends it to the editor with one simple instruction—convert your manuscript to a first grade readability level. The readability score must be first grade. You provided the "high-interest." Now, it's the editor's job to make it low readability. This is where "the ten word chop" comes in to play.

The editor now takes your manuscript and begins the ten-word chop. Starting at the first sentence, the editor counts the first ten words and puts a period after the tenth word (chop!). The editor then starts a brand new sentence beginning with a connector word like "and," "but," or "then." The editor again counts another ten words and chops. This process continues until every sentence in the story is under the ten-word readability requirement for first grade material.

So what's wrong with this? It makes sense, doesn't it? Lowering the number of words in a sentence automatically decreases the readability level of the story. Right? Yes, this is right. Unfortunately, lowering the readability level by changing the grammatical structure of the original sentences does not make the story easier to read. It is actually just the opposite.

Phrases and Clauses are not Sentences

When sentence structures are manipulated to meet an artificial readability standard, they are no longer sentences. They become phrases. Phrases and clauses which begin with "and," "but," and "then"—are not sentences! Phrases are clearly more grammatically complex and less understandable. When we increase the grammatical complexity, we automatically decrease many non-readers' opportunity to make sense out of the material. This process of making sense is known as comprehensibility. For non-readers, comprehensibility, not readability, should be the driving force. Non-readers need to be placed in the most comprehensible materials. Readability formulas prevent this.

In other words, artificially changing the sentence structure of a story to conform to the requirements of a readability formula automatically increases the grammatical complexity of the story and makes the material much harder to read, regardless of how interesting the content. The complex surface structure created by the readability formula actually serves as a barrier that prevents students from accessing the enjoyable deep meaning.

Sentence structure or syntax directly influences comprehension. According to F. J. Di Vestain in, *Language, Learning, And Cognitive Processes*, sentence structure, "...should be considered even in the first primers. Most basal readers (...regardless of grade...) contain stilted sentences that no child (...or student...) would use." Hargis claims that acquisition of syntax follows a developmental sequence, in his book, *Teaching reading to handicapped children* (1982).

Syntactically Challenged

As I previously stated, many older students and students whose first language is not English are "syntactically challenged." They come from homes in which Standard English is not spoken. Because they have little exposure to Standard English, they are denied the opportunity to grasp intuitively the rules of grammar. For these students, these rules must be taught.

"Syntactically challenged" students are limited in their ability to comprehend complex written sentence structures because they cannot relate to the "surface structure" of written text (the way the story is written). They fail to process or gain access to its "deep meaning" (what the story is trying to say). As Harber states, "the continuing development of syntactic structures for all children (especially exceptional children) during their early school years and possibly into adolescence (Wiig & Semel 1974, 1975) must be recognized when planning language and reading instruction. Unfortunately, this important advice is not followed by publishers or developers of reading intervention programs. In fact, it is completely overlooked."

"After examining four series of readers for sequential patterns of increasing syntactic complexity from first through sixth grade, Kachuck (1975) reported that patterns of increases were irregular with no evidence of systematic planning" (Harber, 1979). This same conclusion can still be applied well over a quarter of a century later. Because of the over-reliance on readability formulas, syntactic complexity is overlooked in current reading intervention materials. This is especially true for upper elementary, middle, and high school students.

Ways to Reduce Instructional Complexity

Elisabeth Wiig and Eleanor Semel, co-authors of *Language Assessment & Intervention for the learning disabled*, suggested that the structural complexity of all written materials presented for the language and learning-disabled student to read should be adapted or reduced. Their suggestions are just as strong today. They also suggested the following adaptations for reducing the structural complexity of reading materials: 1) the order-of-mention of critical content words should match the order-of-action, 2) the order or sequence of the individual phrases in sentences should be controlled and adapted to conform to the order of kernel sentences, 3) sentence length should be strictly controlled, 4) sentences with embedded clauses or with nesting of embedded clauses should be rewritten and presented in their logical format, and 5) sentence sequences and paragraphs should have limited pronoun usage.

Using a Syntactic Format

When I created my Failure Free Reading Methodology and instructional materials, I thought it was key to use a "Syntactic Format." I wrote stories in which complex sentence structures were initially kept to a minimum. My initial stories were written in the easiest form of syntactic comprehension—the kernel sentence (simple, active, positive and declarative). Complex structures were introduced only after intensive pre-teaching on the part of the instructor. I never allowed students access to grammatically complex stories without first pre-teaching what these sentence structures meant. Nothing was taken for granted.

I also used the Botel Syntactic Complexity Formula to analyze my materials. The Botel Syntactic Complexity Formula verified that I could control for the use of zero-count and one-count structures (with zero being the easiest and three being the hardest) within a meaningful context. Finally, I never forgot the difference between readability levels (an artificial formula) and comprehensibility levels (how well written and meaningful are the stories for my students).

In summary, the second crucial instructional element for non-readers is sentence structure. Non-readers must be placed in stories that control for complex, passive, negative, and interrogative sentence structures. Sadly, most publishers and authors ignore this entirely.

Story Content—The Third Instructional Element

Students must be able to relate to the content of a story. There must be a good match between what the content is about and what the reader brings to the task. Unfortunately, many students lack the experiences needed to relate to a story.

For example, I was doing a staff-development for a large school system. The community was home to a major state university. The university and the school system had a cooperative agreement to provide services for a developmental preschool. The three and four year old, developmentally disabled students were taught on the university campus. Lunch was provided by the school system. In fact, it was brought over daily to us by Mr. Jones.

One day, the teacher was doing a teaching unit on farm animals. She was telling them about the cow. The students were not aware of what a cow was. Finally, the teacher said, "Class, this is a cow. Does anyone know what we get from a cow?" No one knew. Finally, the teacher said. "We get milk from a cow."

As soon as the teacher said this, a little girl stood up and said "Oh no we don't. We get milk from Mr. Jones!" As far as the little girl was concerned, based on her background and experience, milk did not come from a cow. Milk came from Mr. Jones.

A Good Match

It is critical to have a good match between the story's content and the student's experience. Without such a match, no meaningful reading can take place. Too often, it is assumed the students have the necessary background and experience to relate to the story when they really don't. This is particularly true when the story is written using figurative speech, idiomatic expression, or multiple meaning words.

Our language is rich with figurative speech, idiomatic expressions, and multiple meaning words. We use these parts of the English language everyday. They are as natural as breathing. We take them for granted. The problem is they can be very difficult to understand for non-readers.

Figurative speech or idiomatic expressions or multiple meaning words serve as language roadblocks to reading success. Many students lack the exposure or the ability to comprehend easily this type of language.

Many Students Are Concrete Learners

Many non-readers are concrete learners. They take everything spoken to them on its literal or face value. These students have great difficulty read-

ing between the lines. This is especially true for stories that are rich in figurative speech such as Aesop's Fables and Folklore. These stories can be
particularly difficult. The students can't grasp the underlying meaning of
the stories without a detailed explanation.

Many Students Misinterpret Sarcasm

Many students misinterpret sarcasm. Why? Sarcasm is a form of figurative
speech. Do not use figurative speech if you find that your student is a literal learner. Take my advice and forget sarcasm. It is simply not worth it, as
the following story illustrates.

Meet Johnny

Meet Johnny. Johnny is a bright and very intelligent student. However,
Johnny is also the most disorganized student you will ever meet. He is a bit
scatter-brained when it comes to his organizational skills and it is apparent
when you look at him.

His hair, which is always a mess, points in about six different directions. He looks as if he had his finger caught in a light socket. His shirt is
half out of his pants and he is wearing two completely different colored
socks.

Johnny is about to start his first class of the day.

Meet Mr. Jones

Meet Mr. Jones. A good, hard working teacher, Mr. Jones, is very organized
and he takes great pride in his personal appearance. His well-groomed hair
is perfectly in place, as are all of his clothes. Mr. Jones believes your
appearance expresses your inner value. Mr. Jones is unprepared for the col-
lision that is about to take place—he is about to meet his new first period
class.

Unbeknownst to any of his new students, Mr. Jones is a master of sarcasm. Listen as he attempts to use his highly honed skill on his next target:
"Johnny the Disorganized."

"That's a pretty sharp outfit you're wearing today, my man. You really
look good," Mr. Jones says, with what he thinks is obvious disgust and complete sarcasm.

"Oh wow. Thanks," says Johnny, who, unaware of the biting sarcasm, is excited to learn that Mr. Jones likes something he has done. "I'll tell you what, Mr. Jones, because you like it so much, I'll wear it again for you tomorrow."

Much to Mr. Jones' complete surprise, Johnny did wear the exact same outfit the next day. So much for sarcasm and figurative speech. Stick to saying what you actually mean.

Language Rich with Idioms

Too many of the stories used in reading intervention programs are culturally dependent. Students need to know a lot about the culture if they are to read the story with comprehension. What do I mean by the culture?

The English language is rich with idiomatic expressions. Many of these can be quite confusing for those who are not familiar with the context from which they are based. This is especially true for students with a limited language background or those who are learning English as a second language and therefore, not familiar to the American "culture."

Americans have a tendency to use idioms quite often in everyday speech. For example, consider what a person who is arriving in America for their very first job must think when they are told that the person they replaced, "was fired," or "got the ax."

Stories that are rich in idiomatic expressions and figurative speech can be quite confusing. Be on the lookout for these. Look at your student as you read a story or passage to them. Watch for any confusion in their eyes. Ask questions to be sure they fully understand what these words or phrases mean.

The most important thing to remember is not to take anything for granted. Never assume they understand until they demonstrate an understanding. Never forget that if they can't relate to it, they can't read it.

Do Not be Fooled by High Interest Material

Look out for stories containing lots of multiple meaning words, idiomatic expressions and figurative speech. Again, don't be fooled by the notion of high interest material. Reading is more than high interest. Look beyond the overall story theme or title. Go directly to the actual content and writing style contained in the story. Remember that high interest is useless if the story contains an abundance of multiple-meaning words and figurative speech patterns that will prevent students from relating to the material, as the following example illustrates.

The following sentence is taken from a story written for students who love football. Many would classify it as high-interest. While it might be of high interest, is it written in a manner that is comprehensible? Let's look at one of the sentences in the story.

"The 12-year old quarterback faked a hand-off to his fullback, dropped back three steps, turned, and fired a perfect strike to his left-end, who had cut over behind the opposing secondary."

Yes, football is one topic in which many middle school students would be interested. However, upon closer look, we can soon see that high-interest is not enough. Notice the heavy use of figurative language (faked a hand-off, fired a strike, cut over), the number of words in the sentence (34 words), and the very complex grammatical structure.

This material is far too complex. It would not be easily comprehensible for many non-reading adolescents or adults.

"To succeed at reading, children need a basic vocabulary, some knowledge of the world around them, and the ability to talk about what they know.... Research shows a strong connection between reading and listening" according to *What Works: Research About Teaching And Learning,* published by the U.S. Department of Education (1986). This need only grows as these students enter higher and higher grades where more and more prior knowledge is necessary for success.

"According to this view, called schema theory, readers understand what they read only as it relates to what they already know..." Sweet's (1993, p 3) summary suggests prior knowledge should be looked at in two ways: 1) overall prior knowledge: that which represents the sum of knowledge individuals have acquired as a result of their cumulative experiences both in and out of school and 2) specific prior knowledge: that which represents the particular information an individual needs in order to understand text that deals with a certain topic. Many non-readers are deficient in both of these areas.

We must control for variables within the stories that prevent non-readers from comprehending the story, such as: multiple meaning words, idiomatic expressions, figurative speech, and uncommon names and dates and places. While nothing should be left for granted, it generally is. All too often, non-readers are placed in materials that are too difficult for them to understand. Many stories are either culturally dependent or written on unfamiliar topics. They lack the prior background knowledge to relate to the story.

Failure Free Reading CASE STUDY:
Washington D.C.

Summer Reading Blitz for Special Education

RESEARCH QUESTIONS
Is it possible to accelerate the learning curve of special education (LD, ED, EMR, Medically Involved, ESL) students as measured by:

- Reading Acquisition Rate
- Grade Equivalence
- Effect Size
- NCE's

Is it possible to provide such a high impact solution in a short instructional period of 4 weeks?

SETTING
Washington D.C.
Large urban school district special education centers at 7 different schools
Special education students taught by teachers and assistants during summer school (ED, LD, EMR, Medically Involved, ESL)

POPULATION
Special Education Students ranged from grades 1-8
Special Education Students were identified as those needing the greatest help in reading
Total Special Education Students participating: Approximately 250

AMOUNT OF TRAINING
(3) 3-hour sessions were conducted with the summer school teachers, 3 weeks prior to summer program implementation
(1) 3-hour session was conducted with the teaching assistants, 3 weeks prior to the summer program implementation

AVERAGE LENGTH OF INSTRUCTIONAL TIME
4 weeks
RESULTS
<u>6 of the 7</u> schools conducted Pre and Post Tests using a standardized
measuring instrument
<u>88</u> Special Education students took the Pre and Post Tests
<u>5 out of 6</u> schools **showed growth** in GE
<u>5 out of 6</u> schools **showed growth** in NCE

Prior to treatment:
Students averaged one-half month reading growth for every month in
school

During treatment:
These same students averaged 2 months growth for their month in
Failure Free Reading
<u>400% Increase</u>

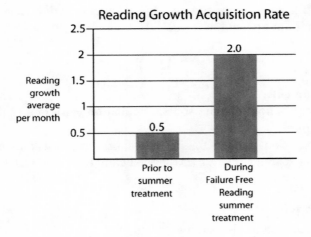

GRADE EQUIVALENCE
Average Grade Level Growth In 1 Month of Treatment
By Individual School

SCHOOL	GE GROWTH (months)
HD Cooke	2.25
Mamie D. Lee	2.80
Prospect	1.90
Sharpe	−1.50
Taft	.33
Moten	5.90

EFFECT SIZE

Measures the performance of treatment in terms of standard deviation
The National Reading Panel suggests the following gauge of strength
   of Effect Size:

A value of: .20 is considered small—little impact

.50 is considered moderate—some impact

.80 is considered large—quite a bit of impact

**Researcher at the University of Missouri reviewed the last 33
   years of research on summer school**
They found the **average Effect Size for all schools to be .26**—very
   little impact

**Failure Free Reading's Effect Size was nearly 3 times (273%)
   greater than typical summer growth**
.26 Average summer Effect Size
.71 *Failure Free Reading summer Effect Size
*Strong Impact

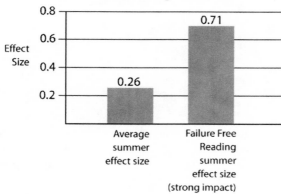

The Average Reading Growth
During Typical Summer School
(according to University of Missouri)
Compared to Failure Free Reading's
Summer Reading Blitz Growth

NCE RESULTS
The Department of Education used the following NCE growth guidelines for Title 1 program yearly evaluations

1–2 NCE's—Positive growth

3–5 NCE's—Very positive growth

6–8 NCE's Extremely positive growth

Failure Free Reading's NCE Results

4 of 6 schools had NCE growth higher than 11 NCE's

Average NCE Growth Per School After 1 Month's Treatment

SCHOOL	NCE GROWTH
HD Cooke	11.42
Mamie D. Lee	32.00*
Prospect	6.31
Sharpe	16.67
Taft	-4.82
Moten	22.51

* Researchers believe this is a spuriously high score

Failure Free Reading's NCE
Average NCE growth during the summer program was 8.5 NCE's

Chapter 5

Five Traditional Reading Approaches

Reading Approaches

Many non-readers are victimized by the limitations of the reading program they are being asked to use. Often, there is a mismatch between the strength of a program (the reason why it is working for the majority of poor and struggling readers in the class) and its weakness (the reason why it is not effective for non-readers).

Let me continue to make this key point, this is not the non-readers' fault. Non-readers are the victims. They are hostages to a "one size fits all" reading intervention program.

Perhaps the following will help illustrate what I mean. How would you answer the following question?

Which of the following is an essential prerequisite for the teaching of reading?

a. knowledge of the letters of the alphabet
b. knowledge of letter sounds
c. ability to see letter patterns within words
d. ability to recognize individual letters and words within a sentence
e. all of the above
f. none of the above

The answer you choose reflects how you view reading. Each response represents a particular theoretical viewpoint of the reading process.

Depending upon which viewpoint you chose, all are accurate—including "f"—none of the above!

As I've already mentioned, reading is one of the most researched areas in the field of education. Literally thousands of studies and articles are done each year on some aspect of reading. Yet, the experts still cannot agree on how reading is to be taught. This is why it is so important that you always remember our key reading research fact: <u>all reading programs work, but not for all students.</u>

Choosing Which Camp is Not Easy

While most experts would agree that reading involves gaining meaning from the printed page, they disagree on how it should be initially taught. The teaching of reading falls into two instructional camps: those who advocate a "skills first" approach and those who believe in a "meaning first" approach. Both camps have strong research; both camps are effective. Choosing which camp to select is not an easy task.

Imagine I am going to teach you how to ride a bike. I am a good researcher as well as a good teacher. I want to use the best "how to ride a bike" teaching method available. I check the research and what I find surprises me. There is actually more than one recognized way to teach you how to ride a bike. There are at least two distinctly different ways. I read more of the research and then I make a decision. Much of my decision is based on fact and data. However, some of my decision is personal and is based on first hand experience. I was taught how to ride using one of these ways and I didn't like it. I always felt there might have been a better way. I always had this nagging doubt that if I had been taught another way it would have made me a much better bike rider.

My attitude toward the choice of which teaching method to use is not uncommon. People promote what has personally worked well for them and they generally stay away from what has personally failed them in the past. I didn't like the way I was taught bike riding so I am going to look elsewhere.

My choice involves taking you to the garage. On the floor of the garage are all the individual pieces of a bike. I inform you that I am going to go over each and every piece lying on the floor. I'll give you the name and purpose of each piece of the bike. Name and purpose. Name and purpose. When I am done, I going to ask you to tell me the name and purpose of each piece of the bike. I also inform you that I don't care if it takes days, weeks, months or years, we will go no further until you can successfully tell me the name and purpose of each bicycle part. Name and purpose. Name and purpose.

How do you think you would do? How do you think you might feel if you could not give me each exact name and purpose of each bike part—no matter how hard you tried? What would it feel like if you went into your second straight year of "name and purpose" drills without ever being allowed to ride a bike because someone thought you couldn't ride because you just couldn't get past this "name and purpose" thing?

What do think the second way of teaching you how to ride might be? I bet you know it. "First put me on the bike!" you might say. "The heck with name and purpose. Let me learn to ride by letting me ride. Give me training wheels, stay close to me and hold the back of my bike's seat as we run down the road. Now there are clearly certain things you might need to do before you put me on that bike, such as making sure I'm on a level road and there are no cars, trees or other obstacles in my path. In addition, you can tell me the name and purpose of the important bike parts such as the steering wheel and the brakes! Later on, we can go over the remaining parts if you think it necessary."

The example I just gave you pertaining to the two ways to teach you how to ride a bike is quite similar to the way we select one of the two primary instructional philosophies involved in teaching someone to read. As you can see, the selection is more than simply saying this is the best method.

The Skills First Approach

Many popular reading theories believe good readers first need to learn letters, letter sounds, and word configurations. These theories are designed to teach these graphic/phonetic prerequisites. Skills first proponents are "bike parts first" reading proponents. Students who master letters and letter sounds are allowed to move on. Those who do not master these skills do not. They are not allowed to proceed to what skills first advocates believe are the more advanced levels like reading fluently. After all, skills first advocates figure, how can a student learn to read fluently when he or she still does not know his/her letters and letter sounds?

The Meaning-First Approach

Proponents of a "meaning-first approach" are 180 degrees removed from their "skills first" adversaries. They are your "get on the bike" believers.

"Meaning firsters" feel that students will learn to read by reading—not by doing skill work. They also believe that skills can be taught at a later stage after students understand the overall reading process (what it feels like to read). Finally, "meaning firsters" actually believe that a skills orientation is counterproductive because it takes valuable time away from actual reading.

Five Basic Reading Approaches

There are mainly five basic reading approaches currently in use: Phonics, Whole Word, Linguistics, Whole Language and Language Experience. Each approach subscribes to one of the two basic instructional philosophies just discussed—"skills first" or "meaning first."

As I have already said, all reading programs work. Every program has value. They have stood the test of time and have tremendous data to support them. No argument here. Each program is effective for the majority but, as we shall soon see, each approach is also very limited for a small but highly significant minority of students.

Why are they limited? Because each approach denies these students simultaneous access to all three sources of information that you now know are critical for their success: repetition, sentence structure and story content. Because of this, each approach uses instructional materials that are too complex for non-readers.

In addition, each approach demands student strength in one particular area. Each does not allow a student to substitute a strength for a weakness in that particular area. In order words, there is no "compensatory mechanism" within each program. All programs are based on the "all or none" principal. Either the students have the necessary strengths needed to succeed or they fail because of the built-in complexity of the instructional materials used in each approach.

One of the Biggest Mistakes

"Built-in complexity?"

Absolutely. I believe that one of the biggest mistakes educators make is their failure to examine the appropriateness of the instructional materials they have selected for their non-readers. In addition, the absolute biggest mistake they make is to assume that these instructional materials are in their simplest form. Nothing could be farther from the truth. These materials are much too complex for non-readers. They are not in their simplest form. The sad thing is, the vast majority of educators do not even know it. For example, how do you think the vast majority of teachers would respond to the following question?

Which is easier for a non-reader: a sentence taken from a pre-primer book (kindergarten) or a sentence taken from a third grade book?

I have found that the vast majority of teachers when asked this question select the sentence taken from the pre-primer. They base their answer on the assumption that because a pre-primer is written for beginning readers, it is written in an easier format. Their answer is incorrect. In many cases, a well-written third grade sentence is much easier to understand than a poorly written pre-primer sentence. The pre-primer material is actually more difficult because the author is forced to comply with the rigid readability requirements that ignore the importance of sentence structure and/or story content.

So let us look at each of the five reading approaches. In particular, let's see how each approach matches up to the key instructional elements essential for a non-reader's success. Specifically, do these approaches contain immediate access to all three crucial instructional elements? In other words, do they provide for abundant contact using stories that control for sentence structure and story content?

Phonics

As I mentioned before, phonics is a term associated with a reading method designed to teach students the rules associated with letter and letter sounds. It is the "heart and soul" of the skills first reading philosophy. Proponents believe there are simply too many words in the English language to memorize. They feel that there are very basic rules that allow students to sound out strange or unfamiliar words. They call this decoding, and once learned, the students will learn beginning and ending sounds, short and long vowels and a variety of helpful ways to attack most of our words successfully. That's a big plus.

What's the minus? The minus is the fact that as I previously mentioned, at least twenty percent of our words are not phonetically correct. They violate the rules of phonics. Without help (in the form of context and sentence structure), many unfamiliar words cannot be figured out without first mastering an elaborate set of exceptions to the rule.

For example, how do you say the following word: "read"? Well, if you use the helpful hint of "When two vowels go a walking (are paired together), the first one does the talking." (says its name). You could conclude that the word is "rEad" as in "Do you like to read at home?" It could also mean the exception to the rule as in: "I read a good book last night."

As I mentioned, proponents of phonics place beginning readers in beginning reading materials that are designed to highlight the phonetic rules. The problem is that in order for the rules to work, these stories must mainly use a phonetically regular vocabulary. While this type of controlled vocabulary makes it easy to apply the rules, (yes, they can figure each word) the stories are not natural and are anything but meaningful.

Consider the following story taken from a once popular SRA Reading series. As I mentioned, once mastered, the student will learn beginning and ending sounds, short and long vowels and a variety of helpful ways to figure out the words in the story.

Six Pet Cats

> Miss Hull had six pet cats—Muff, Cuff, Huff, Puff, Ruff, and E. Nuff.
> Miss Hull had the cats in a pen.
> Miss Hull fed the cats well.
> The cats got big, but the pen did not.
> So the cats did not fit the pen.
> "Jim Bell, at the Red Mill Inn, has a big pen," said Miss Hull. "I will
>   sell the cats to him."

What do you think about the story? Is it easy? Is it cute? Is it comprehensible? For most kids who have a good ear for sounds, it's a piece of cake. No sweat. They'll breeze through it. They can use phonic rules to recognize successfully almost every word in this story.

However, for our Phonetically Deaf students who have a weakness in "hearing the sounds," this is a very complicated and complex piece of material. It is practically unreadable because it does not give them access to other key instructional elements such as abundant repetition, simplified sentence structure and meaningful story content.

Notice the infrequency of many of the words. For example, Muff, Cuff, Huff, Puff, Ruff, E. Nuff, fed, well, so, but, and Jim are presented only once. Remember our "50 or more contacts" rule. Many of our Phonetically Deaf students (PD) will need to see unfamiliar words at least fifty or more times before they can instantly recognize them. Frankly, a one time contact "ain't gonna cut it" with our PD students.

Now let's look at the sentence structure. Our syntactically challenged students, those without an intuitive understanding of the basic rules of grammar, are going to have great difficulty with the way these sentences were written. For example, the first and last sentences in this story are complex sentences; and the words, "So the cats did not fit the pen," are not even in a sentence. They are in a phrase.

Finally, let's go to story content. The names of the cats are not very common names and the reader cannot easily relate to them. Look at the story theme. Most people would not sell their pets just because the pets outgrew their pen. This is quite the opposite of what most, especially young readers, would do under these circumstances. In short, while the words in the story do go together in some sort of adult logic, the story is quite meaningless to a non-reader. It is beyond their realm of experience.

Before I go on, I would like to add one final word about phonics. Let me say this one more time. Phonics is effective and it does have a very important place in the teaching of reading, but, and I stress this, it is not the only way to teach reading.

Whole Word

Whole word is usually the method most associated with a basal reading program. It is usually what people think is a sight or look say approach. In truth, most basal readers employ a variety of word attack procedures. The material is based on a controlled vocabulary. The stories increase in complexity. The beginning stories are believed to be the most basic and in their simplest form. For the majority of students, they are in the simplest form. But, not for some.

For some students, the stories contained in the basal readers are too restrictive. These students are forced to rely almost exclusively on visual information (the print on the page) because the beginning stories ignore the importance of sentence structure and story content. Consider the following example.

The following story is taken from a popular basal reading series. The title of the group of stories in the book is "Bears." The first story, "'I Will Go" consists of drawings of three birds sitting on a tree branch. The birds are talking among themselves.

> "I will go."
> "Will you go?"
> "I will go."
> "We will go."
> "Will you go?"

"I will not go."
"I will go in."

At this point, two of the three birds are shown flying off to a birdhouse while the third bird appears to be headed for a tree hole, only to find a squirrel blocking his way.

The bird then says:

"I will not go in."
"You go in."
"I will go."

Three squirrels are now on the next page gathering nuts. The story ends when one squirrel says:

"We will go in."

Yes, the story is very repetitious. There are a large number of contacts with the text, but it lacks comprehensibility. It is very confusing and makes little sense. While this section is titled "Bears," the first story is about birds!

The pictures are confusing and the story lacks any meaningful content. On the last page, the bird is shown flying between the squirrels below, and two other birds who are sitting in a birdhouse above. There is no indication in what direction the bird is flying or whom the bird is talking to: the other birds or the squirrels.

There is also heavy use of the pronouns: I, you, and we. Studies have shown using pronouns in place of proper nouns, especially for non-readers, dramatically decrease a student's ability to comprehend a story.

The sentence structure is also too complex. Beginning and remedial reading material must use basic sentence structures. Many factors affect comprehensibility. The simplest sentence structures to comprehend (as I mentioned earlier) are simple, active, positive, and declarative. Sentences that deviate from this pattern reduce their comprehensibility. They are less understandable.

The sentences in our example are not in the simplest sentence structure. The second sentence on the first page ("Will you go?") is an interrogative sentence. The same holds true for the second sentence on the next page. In addition, the sentence immediately following it is negative. ("I will not go.")

Given the complexity of the story content and sentence structure in this material, non-readers have only text information available. They have to memorize the words on the page in order to survive. Access to other forms of information is denied. Success is based on memory. Students with poor visual memory skills will fail in this type of approach.

Linguistic Based Approaches

Linguistic based approaches also concentrate on print recognition. They are concerned with the identification of letter patterns. Students are taught the basic letter patterns or word families and then shown how to vary these patterns to make more and more words. For example, the instructor might say to his class, "a-k-e is pronounced ake, what happens when we put an **l** in front of ake or a **b** or a **c** or an **m**?"

Students are asked to read sentences and stories based on the most common word family letter patterns: such as "Dan can fan Nan." As expected, sentence structure and story content are not controlled for in this approach (what is meaningful about a sentence such as "the fat cat sat on a mat?"). These types of meaningless sentences deny students access to the use of context. This again causes students to rely almost exclusively on one single source of information—the graphic/phonetic information available on the page.

Whole Language

Whole language is a literature based reading program. There are no basal readers. No controlled vocabulary. No prerequisite set of materials the students must master. Proponents of whole language believe that it most closely resembles the real world of reading. A world where students can read for enjoyment and from a broad variety of contents. Proponents believe in exposing all students to a variety of different stories and genres.

Proponents of whole language stress reading as a meaning based process. Complex sentence structures and figurative language usage are not controlled. Judging from the success achieved and the large and growing number of proponents, this approach has been very successful.

But not completely successful.

Opponents of a whole language approach cite a lack of organization and structure as a chief drawback. The approach is highly implicit. Students are not formally taught specific skills. They believe that students will learn to read by reading. While an excellent idea for experienced readers, many stories are too complex for many beginning and struggling readers, particularly our ED (Environmentally Denied) and LD (Language Deprived) students, who have a limited experiential and language base and especially too difficult for non-readers.

Consider the following excerpt from the big book, *When Goldilocks Went to the House of the Bears* (Green, Pollock and Scarffe).

> When Goldilocks went
> to the house of the bears,
> Oh, what did her blue eyes see?
> A bowl that was BIG
> A bowl that was small,
> A bowl that was tiny,
> And that was all.
> She ate from them, 1. 2. 3.

Is this a meaningful story written in a simple sentence structure? Yes, for some, but not for all. For some, the sentence structure is complex and unpredictable. The story is confusing (what is the difference between a small bowl and a tiny bowl?). In addition, "And that was all" is not a sentence. It is a phrase, which automatically increases sentence complexity and hinders comprehensibility.

Finally, look at the last sentence, "She ate from them, 1.2.3." Imagine covering up the last part of the final sentence. Could anyone easily be able to anticipate "1.2.3." as logically coming next in the story? I don't think so.

While the story is very cute and fun to read as an adult or by an adult to young children, it is very complicated for our ED and LD non-readers.

Summary

Until recently, most reading programs fell into one of two broad classifications known as the "bottom-up" or the "top-down" models. The bottom-up model views the reading process as a series of discrete stages. Proponents believe reading must first concentrate on the perception of letters and words. In other words, students are expected to master their letters and letter sounds before they are placed in more meaningful reading materials. These are your skills first people.

Advocates of the top-down model believe reading is more than letter and word identification. They see reading as a higher-level cognitive process, which requires the successful interaction between the reader and the printed material.

Top-down theorists believe readers do not read letter by letter or word by word because it impedes comprehension. They believe students must learn that reading is a process in which meaning is gained from the page. These are your whole language and language experience people.

So who's right? The answer is both.

Students do need to know how to recognize individual words and letters, but they also need to work in meaningful and age-appropriate reading materials from the very start. The fluent reader must be able to compute many different kinds of information in a relatively short period. They need to be able to access simultaneously the information available in print, sentence structure and story content from the very start.

Why? Because research has shown that denying students access to all three elements increases the complexity of the task. Reading becomes much harder to accomplish.

As you can see, all five approaches have both strengths and weaknesses. They all work, but not for all students. This is especially true for non-readers. All of these approaches are too complex for non-readers.

Noted Canadian reading researcher, Keith E. Stanovich (1980), mentions a compensatory component. According to this, readers with a weakness in one area will use information from another to compensate. In other words, students with poor word recognition skills will use context to figure out the word. Unfortunately, existing remedial and traditional reading methods and materials do not control for the simutaneous acces to all three sources of information.

As Hargis stated in his 1982 book, *Teaching Reading to Handicapped Children*, "Teachers often complain about inconsistent responses from students who have severe reading problems. 'They seem to know the words one day but not the next.' This observation reflects a problem for children not introduced to words in meaningful context with sufficient repetition and who have not yet been able to do any meaningful reading—often after years in school. They fall into this predicament because there are no published materials with sufficient controls to permit meaningful activities."

In other words, students who had severe reading problems were not being given the opportunity to demonstrate that they could actually compensate by substituting an inner strength with a known weakness. Current reading materials actually prevented such a compensation from taking place by denying them access to the simultaneous utilization of text repetition, basic sentence structure and highly meaning context.

Until Now...

When I failed to find an approach that controlled for the simultaneous utilization of text repetition, basic sentence structure and meaningful story content, I created it and the reading materials that went with it. Quite honestly, it wasn't easy staring at graded word lists in alphabetical order and creating meaningful stories that controlled for multiple meaning words, idiomatic expressions, uncommon names, dates and places that were written in a basic sentence structure. It didn't happen overnight. In addition, I developed my own methodology and infused that into my new reading program.

After years of research and countless classrooms, I had a huge decision to make. Did I have the guts to go out there and truly practice what I preached? I thought long and hard, spoke to my wife, and we decided to bite the bullet: We started our own company. This was a scary thing to do, venture out into the great unknown. We had our family to think about, but this was an important risk that had to be taken. If I didn't speak about what I had seen, experienced, and learned, then who else would? So I decided to work hard and simply see what would happen.

I was amazed at the results. The number of non-readers reached was astounding. Most were finally experiencing a successful reading experience for the very first time in their life. It was amazing to see that students who had seen nothing but failure were reading fluently with full comprehension from age-appropriate materials. Maybe the best side effect of the program was the students' improvement in self-esteem! It was dramatic. We started the business out of the spare bedroom in our house, now we are in countless schools helping thousands of students across the nation. We have been blessed. Happily, the students' new found success hasn't stopped. It was and still is "failure free."

During the past year alone, I have given reading demonstrations in such diverse educational sites as federally funded reading programs in the heart of the Mississippi Delta, inner city schools in Detroit, maximum-security prisons in South Carolina, and parent preschool literacy projects in Alabama, as well as in inner city New York and Los Angeles.

I will only make these demonstrations under one condition, and I make only one claim. The condition? I'll only work with the worst readers at the site. The claim? If they don't have a successful reading experience in less than 30 minutes, I'll walk out the door and you won't hear from me again.

I haven't walked yet...

What's even more startling is the level of performance. No watered down childish material. Using the Failure Free Reading Methodology allows non-reading adolescents and adults to read successfully at an instructional reading level of 7th to 12th grade from the very first lesson! Did I cure them in thirty minutes? No, but I did give them hope. I showed them that they could read faster, comprehend higher and do much more!

The testimonials keep pouring in. Testimonials from hard-nosed professionals who have seen and heard it all and are not easily impressed. Teachers write about how their Down's Syndrome students beg to read every day from the program. Parents talk about how their children have shown more growth in two weeks using the program than they did after a full year in a highly touted, considerably more expensive program.

Please look at the parent and teacher testimonials found throughout the book, as well as the case studies on schools that have used Failure Free Reading. These are personal stories and experiences that people have been kind enough to share, these remind me why we have to help every single child to overcome their obstacles and learn to read.

Aside from what I've just mentioned, Failure Free Reading is different because it is the first reading program to control for the three elements known to be crucial for non-readers' reading success: adequate repetition, simplified sentence structure and meaningful story content. It reduces reading to its simplest form. As the following chart illustrates, no other reading approach for non-readers controls for all three.

Methodology	Controls For Graphic Info.	Controls For Sentence Structure	Controls For Story Content
Phonetic	YES	NO	NO
Whole Word	NO	NO	NO
Linguistic	YES	NO	NO
Whole Language	NO	NO	YES
Lang. Experience	NO	NO	YES
Failure Free	YES	YES	YES

Chapter 6

Putting The Failure Free Reading Methodology Into Play

This chapter of the book has two segments. The first segment deals with finding or creating comprehensible reading material. The second segment describes the Failure Free Reading Methodology and is broken into a series of sequential instructional presentations. As I mentioned, the Failure Free Reading Methodology will work. Non-readers should not fail if you faithfully follow the directions contained in this chapter about the Failure Free Reading instructional procedure and the process for selecting comprehensible reading materials.

The Failure Free Approach to Reading

As I've already mentioned, the Failure Free Reading approach reduces reading to its simplest form by controlling for the three instructional elements crucial to reading success: repetition, sentence structure and story content. It also takes into account the three characteristics of non-readers: phonetically deaf, environmentally denied, and language deprived. The methodology is designed to provide a highly structured language development lesson that teaches word recognition, comprehension and fluency.

The primary purpose of this book is to give you a basic understanding of this unique reading process as it pertains to non-readers. It is also designed to give you hope. Non-readers can be helped, regardless of past performance.

I called my approach Failure Free Reading because it uses a "failure free" format. I have been working on Failure Free Reading for well over thirty years. It has been extensively field-tested across the nation. There are currently over 80 studies involving over 8,000 students and seven published articles in international and national educational research journals. The students cut across grade levels and classifications. All students had been identified as the poorest readers in their building or district. Most were called non-readers. Here are some of the different populations Failure Free Reading has served: non-English speaking, severely learning disabled, mild and moderate mental retardation, autistic, deaf, hearing impaired, emotionally disturbed, brain injured students and adults, elementary, middle and high schools students as well as incarcerated youth and adults.

Surprisingly, Failure Free Reading has had an incredible 85% and higher success rate for improving the reading comprehension and fluency rate of non-readers reading as low as 0.0 and testing well below the 15th percentile in reading comprehension. Frankly, the vast majority of non-readers do not fail when the Failure Free Reading Methodology is followed. As one teacher answered when asked, "When does Failure Free Reading not work?"

"When you don't take it out of its wrapper!" the teacher replied.

Even more dramatic is the speed at which Failure Free Reading works. You can expect to see dramatic improvement in fluency, comprehension and confidence within the first thirty minutes. That's right you will see a dramatic and immediate response to treatment. While we won't cure a non-reader in thirty minutes, you will see improvement that will astound you and make a difference in the confidence of the student. Even better, it will be at levels that you probably thought were impossible. My goal is always to have non-readers reading fluently from grade level or higher. In most cases, they can experience this during the very first lesson—regardless of their prior reading ability.

Over the past twenty years, Failure Free Reading has become the leading reading alternative for our nation's non-readers. Failure Free Reading has been: 1) featured on national TV (PBS NewsHour with Jim Lehrer), 2) mentioned on national radio (The Tom Joyner Show), 3) written about in international and national reading research journals, 4) designated as "a promising practice in reading" by the Education Commission of the States and 5) selected for inclusion as one of only four national reading intervention models in the Power4Kids study (jointly sponsored by the Hahn and Heinz Foundations along with the United states Department of Education). Power4Kids is the largest controlled longitudinal reading research study in United States history.

So all right, you might say. Failure Free Reading works! No doubt about it. Now tell me why. Why does Failure Free Reading work after all other programs have failed the non-reader?

As I stressed repeatedly throughout this book, the Failure Free Reading Methodology is based on the three most important words in the teaching of reading comprehension: reading is relating!

Non-readers must be able to relate to what they read. They must be able to relate to the words, phrases, the sentence structure and the story's content. When they can relate, successful reading will take place. When they can't relate, reading failure will occur.

Segment I:

Selecting Appropriate Reading Material That Fits The Failure Free Reading Methodology

The process for selecting comprehensible reading materials is designed to allow non-readers to improve their reading by reading. It does this by helping you locate or create meaningful reading material students can easily read with little or no assistance.

According to, *What Works: Research About Teaching and Learning*, the federal publication on research about teaching and learning, students "…improve their reading ability by reading a lot. Reading achievement is directly related to the amount of reading…[students]…do in school and outside," (p. 11, 1986). Twenty years later, this notion still rings true and is one of the cornerstones of Failure Free Reading: to allow non-readers to have successful reading experiences with age-appropriate comprehensible reading materials. The key word is "comprehensible."

Your Role in The Teaching of Reading

Your attitude and expectations are critical to the success of the program. Your primary role is to give non-readers an opportunity to experience directly the reading process. Remember: anyone can learn how to read. That's right; anyone can learn how to read up to their potential, as long as they 1) are placed in comprehensible reading materials, 2) practice the

Failure Free Reading Methodology, and 3) are taught by someone who believes in their ability to achieve.

This chapter will provide you with the knowledge of how to locate or create comprehensible reading materials. You have to provide the trust and high expectations. It's up to you to present this material in a non-threatening and highly reinforcing atmosphere. You must believe. You must forget their past and prior performance. You have to set high goals and expectations for your non-reader. You must trust in the learner's capacity to learn.

Next, you must follow the Failure Free Reading Methodology. The Failure Free Reading Methodology reduces reading to its simplest form by controlling for the three instructional elements crucial to reading success: repetition, sentence structure and story content. It also takes into account the three characteristics of non-readers: phonetically deaf, environmentally denied, and language deprived. The methodology is designed to provide a highly structured language development lesson that teaches word recognition, comprehension and fluency. While it is acceptable to adapt Failure Free Reading to meet specific content demands, it must be done within limits. Let student behavior be your guide. If they experience success and show growing confidence, continue with what you are doing. If they experience difficulty, check to make sure you have followed all of the directions and are using the most comprehensible material. This is what we are about to discuss in great detail.

You are the agent of change. You are going to give students the opportunity to experience age-appropriate reading. They will read fluently with full comprehension. This is your gift to them. You are the key ingredient. This will happen as long as you: 1) trust in non-readers' capacity to learn, 2) place them in the most comprehensible reading material and 3) follow the Failure Free Reading Methodology.

Let's Move on With What We Know

As I stated earlier, advocates of the interactive-reading model believe reading is an interactive process involving the reader and the printed page. This is especially true for non-readers. The interactive-reading model is based on the successful utilization of three specific types of information: 1) the print on the page, 2) the grammar or sentence structure and 3) the content of the story.

When control of one or more of these elements is missing, the more difficult it will be for non-readers to read fluently with full comprehension. It is one of the chief reasons why they are non-readers. Given their characteristics, they need the simultaneous access to all three types of information.

While we can't easily change or eliminate their characteristics, we can change the stories non-readers are asked to read. We can make these stories more repetitious, using a more basic sentence structure that controls for culturally neutral content such as eliminating the use of uncommon names, dates, places and idiomatic expressions. This is what I mean by comprehensibility.

Not all books are written equally. Some are much more comprehensible than others are for non-readers of any age. The more comprehensible they are, the less reading failure will take place.

Putting It All Together

Are you ready to help someone learn to read? You are probably saying to yourself, "Am I really ready? Can I do this? Do I have the skills to help someone to read?"

The answer is yes, yes, and YES! All you have to do is follow the directions. Don't worry. Relax. You're going to do just fine.

Step One: Finding Appropriate Material

The first step is to find appropriate reading material. What do I mean by appropriate? Appropriate means comprehensible. Comprehensible, as we have already mentioned, means controlling for repetition, sentence structure and story content.

Where can you find comprehensible material? You can borrow it, you can create it, or you can buy it.

Borrowing The Material

Let's look at "borrowing." Start at your school or local library. Pick a topic in which your student is interested. Be sure it's something he/she (not you) will like and are familiar with. Remember: you need to have a good fit between what your student already knows about the topic and the information contained in the story. The more they know prior to reading it, the easier the material will be to read as they read it. Don't assume they know and don't rely simply on basis of the title.

Next, open the book. Look at the sentences and words used in the sentences. Ask yourself the following: how repetitious are the words and sentences in the chapters of the story? Do I see key words or terms repeated throughout the chapters or the story? How often are new words introduced? How many times are these words repeated?

Repetition of key terms and phrases dramatically increases reading ability. Repetition is important. Don't bring your feelings into it. Don't think about how boring repetition can be. Change your perspective. Try to find the most repetitious material. You must quit thinking as an adult who knows how to read and is turned off by so much repetition. Yes, this might be very boring to you. It is not boring to your non-reader.

Remember, non-readers need this constant contact and practice in order to develop instant word recognition. This only comes with exposure. Don't worry about yourself. Take a deep breath and watch in delight as they start to read these same words repeatedly with more and more success. I know it may sound like a cliché but it is truly amazing to watch as a person learns how to read.

Ignore Cute Books

Ignore cute books. These books generally contain constantly changing characters, words and terms that are briefly introduced and then ignored throughout the rest of the story. What might look cute and charming from an experienced reader's viewpoint can be very complicated to the non-reader. Check to see if the next part of the story or chapter or paragraph reinforces the words previously introduced. If they do, keep the book and move on. If they don't, close the book and look for something else.

It's time to check sentence structure. First, ask yourself, "Are these sentences complete?" Stay away from stories where the sentences begin with: AND, BUT, OR or THEN. Why? They are not complete sentences, and they will cause a reading breakdown. Are there abundant quotation marks? Lots of pronouns? Both of these characteristics decrease comprehensibility.

Now check the complexity of the sentences. How many words are in the sentence? Generally speaking, young children can comprehend 5-8 words per sentence. Elementary students can comprehend between 8-12 words per sentence. Adolescents and adults can comprehend 12-16 words per sentence.

Stay away from sentences that are in 25-40 words in length. They are usually much too hard for the non-reader. Don't rely exclusively on word length. Sometimes a compound sentence connected by "and" will be much easier to read than a less lengthy but more complex sentence with embedded clauses and phrases.

Consider the following, "The big dog ate the bag of dog food. Then the dog went to sleep under the tree." Yes, this meets the traditional readability word count criteria of less than nine words each. However, it does not meet the comprehensibility criteria of using two complete sentences. The second group of words is not a sentence. It is a phrase starting with "then." This is a good example of how one longer sentence such as, "The big dog ate the bag of dog food and went to sleep under the tree," is much more comprehensible than two smaller combination of sentences and phrases. In other words, this illustrates how sentences, which are considered too difficult, based on traditional readability formulas, can actually be easier to understand for non-readers. This is one of the reasons that Failure Free Reading, which is based exclusively on comprehensibility, can have non-readers reading from material four and five grade levels higher.

Look at Order of Mention

Next, look at the "order-of-mention" in the sentences. Stay with sentences in which the "order-of-mention" matches the traditional "order-of-action." For example, the sentence, "Before you go out to play, clean up your room," would be much easier to read and comprehend if it were written in its logical order of mention, "Clean up your room before you go out to play."

Now, look at the tense in which the story is written. Sentences written in the active tense, "The man drove the car," are much easier to read and comprehend than those written in the passive, "The car was driven by the man." Watch out for an abundant use of negative words and phrases. Negative sentences and phrases such as, "which is not the car selected," cut down on comprehensibility. The brain actually processes negative sentences more like algebraic equations.

Hope You Are Lucky

Hopefully and if you are very lucky, you should have a book that is written on a topic your student likes and can easily relate to. It should be fairly repetitious in its use of words and written in a basic and predictable sentence patterns. There should be a minimum amount of complex sentences and phrases and an average number of words in each sentence. Books like these do exist but they are not in abundance. They will not be easy to find. Be patient.

Now it's time to check the story's content. First, check the vocabulary. Does the story use words within your student's vocabulary? Is there a minimum use of personal names, pronouns, places and dates? Are the names familiar to your student's ear? Are the places and dates within your student's realm of experience? If you answer yes to these questions, move on. If you answer no, find another book.

Now look at the story's content. What is the story about? What is the message the author is trying to convey? Is it about a topic to which your student can relate? Too often, the story theme is not in your student's realm of experience, or the story jumps from one theme to another. This is especially true in traditional reading material. If your answers are mainly positive, that's great. Continue with the book. If the book does not meet much of these criteria, do not use the book.

Check the Story's Flow

Finally, check to see if the story flows in a logical manner. Does the preceding sentence or paragraph prepare you for the next sentence or paragraph? Look at the order of the sentences within the paragraphs. Do they make sense? Do they all relate to one another? Are they on the same theme? Does the story make sense?

Let's look at the following example:

> "John is going to play with his best friend Paul. He is going to meet him outside. Then they will go over to the playground. John's mother is baking a cake."

How would you rank this paragraph? Is it well written and comprehensible or poorly written and confusing? I believe this is an example of a paragraph to avoid. It is too confusing. Look at the second sentence: "He is going to meet him outside." Who is "he"—John or Paul? Is John going to meet Paul or is Paul going to meet John? The use of pronouns can be very confusing.

Now look at the third sentence: "Then they will go over to the playground!" You know what is wrong? That's right, it is not a sentence. It is a clause that begins with the word "then." More importantly, look at the last sentence: "John's mother is baking a cake." This sentence does not belong here. It does not relate to the theme contained in the other three sentences. What does "John's mother is baking a cake" have to do with the first three thoughts? While "John's mother is baking a cake" is a "good" sentence (easy to read because it is simple and declarative), it shouldn't be placed after the other three sentences because it doesn't fit logically.

How could anyone (yourself included) predict the writer would write, "John's mother is baking a cake," as the final sentence in this paragraph? It doesn't fit. The first three sentences are about John and Paul and that they are meeting each other to go outside and play. Where does baking a cake fit in with meeting a friend and going outside? While you may think this example is rare, it is actually a perfect example of writing that happens all the time.

Paragraphs like the previous example are found frequently in many instructional reading materials. Why? Because the authors are trying to introduce as many new words as possible using traditional readability guidelines. Unfortunately, most authors forget the importance of the phrase "within a meaningful context." Most of these stories are not meaningful.

Watch out for material that jumps around too much within the story. When the story moves from one topic to another and then another with no consistent theme, close the book. If you continue to use the book, be prepared to explain it in much greater detail so that it makes sense to your student. Your student must understand what they are reading; comprehension is key.

Watch Out For The "Classics"

Don't be fooled by how simple a story appears or how much you loved the story when you were a child. This is especially true for the so-called "classics." Many times these classics (stories people rave about) are not what they appear to be, as the following example from Dr. Seuss,' *Green Eggs and Ham,* illustrates.

"I loved, *Green Eggs and Ham*," said the worried parent. "And yet my child hates it. How could anyone hate *Green Eggs and Ham*? It's just so much fun to read. It's so cute."

Now let me set the story straight, *Green Eggs and Ham* is a wonderful book, but it may not be appropriate for a struggling or non-reader. Yes, *Green Eggs and Ham* is cute, but remember what I said about cute. What is cute to an adult can be painfully complex to non-readers. This book may be especially difficult if you are attempting to have them read it by themselves. While these stories might be quite enjoyable when they are read aloud, it would never be my choice for independent reading as the following excerpt illustrates.

If you are not familiar with the story line of this book, it centers on a character called the "Grinch" and his relationship with another character called "'Sam-I-am." "Sam-I-am" is annoying the Grinch. The story starts out like this:

"That Sam-I-am!
That Sam-I-am!
I do not like
that Sam-I-am!"

Look at the complex sentence structure the story begins with (as well as a very unusual name). How many students would be able to anticipate a name like Sam-I-am? Yes, I know it's designed learn to recognize critical words by themselves. What good is recognizing the word if what you read does not make any sense?

The story continues with the question:

"Do you like green eggs and ham?"

Who ever heard of green eggs and ham? Remember: Forget the notion of "cute." Don't confuse cute with simple. The Grinch goes on by saying:

"I do not like them,
Sam-I-am.
I do not like
green eggs and ham."

Sam-I-am continues in the story by asking the Grinch:

"Would you eat them here or there?"

What is the "them?" Are we still talking about "green eggs and ham"? Who could anticipate the sentence: "would you eat them here or there?"

"I would not like them
here or there.
I would not like them
anywhere.
I do not like
green eggs and ham.
I do not like them,
Sam-I-am."

Now look at the next statement by Sam-I-am:

"Would you like them
in a house?
Would you like them
with a mouse?"

How can your student anticipate these last two sentences? Yes, they rhyme, however, they do not make sense. They are not comprehensible.

Am I putting down Dr. Seuss' *Green Eggs and Ham*? No, I am not. I am only trying to show how some books, while fun to read to a child or student, are not (regardless of what the publisher claims) easy to read independently. When you see this happening, close the book. Don't use it for initial reading instruction. This is not an example of a comprehensible book. Remember, when stories are not comprehensible, students have to rely exclusively on memory. Sadly, those with the strongest visual memory win.

As you can see, finding a comprehensible book will not be easy. It will require energy and compromise. Don't give up. These books do exist and now that you are armed with this new knowledge, you will find them.

Listening Comprehension

Once you find what appears to be a good, well-written, comprehensible book, it is time check to see if there really is a "good fit" between the book and your student. How do you do that? It is very easy. Read parts of the book aloud. Watch your student's reaction to the book. Check the eyes. Does he/she appear to understand the story's theme? Ask questions about what you have just read. Did he/she give the correct responses?

Listening comprehension (what your student understands when you read to him/her aloud) determines what your student can read for meaning. Students cannot read what they cannot understand. Listening comprehension helps determine their level of comprehension. If your students can understand what you read to them, they can probably read this material with your assistance. If they are easily confused, close the book. Don't use it.

Congratulations! You've found a suitable book. You've checked its comprehensibility and determined that it's at your student's level of listening comprehension. The sentence structure looks good. The story content makes sense. It is repetitious and highly comprehensible. That's great. You're ready to use this book with the Failure Free Reading Methodology.

Creating a Story

What if you cannot find a suitable book for your student? What if they are all too difficult? Are you out of luck? No way! You still have two very good options left: create it or buy it.

Creating a story that your students can read is an excellent option if you have the time and energy to do so. If you do, remember to follow these key steps:

1. Choose a topic your student likes.
2. Choose a topic to which your student can relate.
3. Write in a basic sentence structure.
4. Repeat key words and phrases often.
5. Write an orderly and logical story.
6. Minimize the names of people and places, pronouns, and idioms.
7. Make the sentences and story comprehensible.

Buying a Story

Don't have the time and energy to create a story? You might want to consider buying commercially prepared material that fits all of these standards—material like Failure Free Reading.

The Failure Free Reading Instructional Procedure

So now you are ready to teach a student to read. How well you do in helping your student is based on three things: preparation, management and adherence. Remember the following:

1. Prepare your students.
2. Make the lessons manageable.
3. Follow the methodology.

Preparation

I know you are probably very scared over the thought of teaching a nonreader how to read. That's ok. It's normal. Never forget, that your student is probably twice as frightened over the thought of failing in front of you.

You are a very important person in your student or child's eyes. They want to impress you. They want you to be proud of them. They don't want to disappoint you—regardless of how they might protest. This is especially true for an adolescent or an adult.

When it comes to reading, non-readers don't feel good about themselves. They are embarrassed. They've failed before and probably expect to fail again. They are in need of an immediate attitude adjustment. Fortunately, your students are only minutes away from their first reading success. But before you can get them there, you've got to calm them down. Take the pressure off them. Get them to relax. But how?

I have always found honesty is still the best policy. Tell your students you are trying a new approach that guarantees success at very high levels. "They say this really works!" Let your students know that you're scared too: "I'm really nervous. I hope I do this right." Let your students know you need their help: "Would you let me try this approach with you and see what happens?"

Set your standard: "I think that this is just what we've been looking for to help you become a very good reader." Do not aim too high at first: "I know great reading won't come overnight. It takes practice. But we have to start somewhere. Let's give it a try."

Praise, Pride, and Confidence

Finally remember: praise, pride and confidence are the cornerstones to success. Look for every opportunity to praise your students from the very beginning. "I am so proud of your courage to try something new. You are fantastic."

Watch as they start to develop pride when they realize that someone really cares and wants them to do well. Watch their confidence build as you continue to psychologically pat them on the back through the beginning process. Always remember that "Little Train Philosophy." I think I can. I think I can.

Keeping it Manageable

Don't ask for too much in the first few lessons. Give them manageable chunks. Let them bask in their initial success. Don't push too fast. Do a couple of paragraphs at first. Don't try to do an entire story in one sitting. Remember, you didn't start out in this life running. You first had to learn how to walk, and you learned how to walk one step at a time. There will be a tremendous amount of new information in the first few paragraphs. We just don't want to overload them with too many full pages and chapters.

There will be plenty of time to go faster later as your student becomes more comfortable with the process and develops confidence. Soon you will be expected to push. You will be expected to give them what they need. Now is not the time. Keep it manageable during those first few lessons.

Follow The Failure Free Reading Methodology

Now that you have comprehensible material, how do you present it in the most meaningful fashion? This is where the Failure Free Reading Methodology comes into play. The specific instructional procedure for Failure Free Reading is as follows: Preview, Listen, Present, Read, and Review. The following is an explanation of each.

Preview

This consists of "setting the stage" for the student and includes a brief discussion that will prepare the student for the story you are about to read. This is a critical part of the process. Never start out cold. Don't start out by simply reading aloud or expecting your student to open the book and begin. We have to make sure that we are language teachers first and reading teachers second. Every action we take is to expand and develop your student's language base. Language. Language. Language.

Start out by explaining. Make sure the stage is set for good reading. Prepare him/her for the central theme or topic of the story. Why do you want to set this stage? Because reading is relating. You want to make sure that your student can relate to what he/she is about to read. That's why you must look at every aspect of the story, from its central theme to the vocabulary and phrases contained in each of its paragraphs. Don't leave anything to chance. Never assume.

Be Positive

You must be positive. The story you are going to use must be either something that is in your student's realm of experience or something that you can easily tie into their realm of experience. Imagine standing with both of your hands straight out in front of you. Keep both hands as level as possible. Do not let one hand rise higher than the other. Now imagine that one hand represents the content of the story that you as the teacher (or as the parent acting as the teacher) are about to present. The second hand represents what your student knows about critical aspects of this particular story. Now imagine that the teacher hand starts to rise while the student hand starts to drop. A gap begins to form. This gap is the teacher / student frustration level. The teacher frustration level occurs when a teacher tries to present or explain content that is too difficult for the student's current knowledge base. While it is very acceptable to have the teacher hand a little bit higher, there is a point where going too high has too many negative effects on the part of both the teacher and the students.

Good teaching is bridging the gap between what the student currently knows and what he/she needs to know in order to make sense out of the story. If you can't bridge this gap through a discussion of the story's central theme and an explanation of its vocabulary and phrases (in ways that make sense to your student), forget this story or content for now.

Read Aloud

Now it's time to read part of the story aloud to your students. You do this for three reasons: 1) to start to make them familiar with the content of the story, 2) to serve as a model for what good reading sounds like, and 3) to expand their vocabulary and knowledge base.

I cannot over emphasize the importance of reading aloud to students. The research is quite clear on this issue. Noted language researcher Steven A. Stahl, in his book, *Vocabulary Development*, states that students…"can learn words as efficiently from having stories read to them as they can from reading stories themselves. For example, Stahl, Richek, and Vandevier (1990) found that sixth graders learned about as many word meanings from a single listening as they would learn from a single reading. This was especially true for children with lower vocabulary knowledge," (p13). Speak clearly and read with good cadence and expression. Language. Language. Language. Never assume.

Discuss and Question

This component is designed to further insure your student can understand all aspects of the story's theme and vocabulary. A story that is above his/her level of comprehension is of no value. Listening comprehension is an excellent measurement of whether the passage you are reading is suitable. If your student understands the story when it's read aloud to him/her, he/she will probably be able to read it with your assistance. Questioning is an excellent way to monitor story comprehension.

Three Kinds of Questions

The Failure Free Reading Methodology uses three kinds of questions to check and enhance your student's level of understanding. These questions are factual, inferential, and leading.

A factual question asks your students to give an accurate and exact answer about something they have just heard in the story. Factual questions cover specific story content. Questions such as "Name three things the man did," or "What happened after the accident?" or "When did the train leave the station?" are all examples of factual questions. The answers have to be exact.

Inferential and leading questions are used to increase your students' ability to make meaningful context-based predictions. They also promote higher-order thinking skills. Inferential questions are open-ended. This means that your students are not expected to give an exact answer. The questions are designed to have your students think about all possible answers and expand their thinking skills.

Questions such as, "Why do you think?" or "How would you have done it?" are all examples of inferential questions. Remember, there are no right or wrong answers. Don't put them down for what they say or think.

Leading questions are designed to help your students make meaningful predictions on upcoming words or phrases using context. "What word makes sense?" or "What did you think comes next?" are examples of leading questions.

Read Again

This part of the procedure starts the formal reading fluency process for your students. You are the role model. You want to demonstrate to them what good fluent reading looks and sounds like. You are to read each sentence aloud to your students as they watch you. Ask if they would like to hear the sentence again before they try to read it by themselves. There is no limit on the number of times they can ask to have you read it. Remember to read with enthusiasm and expression. This is a technique called "repeated readings." It is an excellent research documented way to promote fluency. The only caution concerning "repeated readings," centers on the use of comprehensible material. Many commercial programs based on "repeated readings" ignore the use of meaningful stories. Repeated reading will fail when comprehensible passages are ignored.

Now, it's your student's time to read the sentences aloud. Don't let him/her fail. Introduce him/her to unfamiliar words. Do not ask him/her to stop and "study each word" or any other word attack procedure during this fluency stage. Don't worry if your student needs repeated assistance with this part of the process. This is just the first step; independent fluency will come later.

Reinforcement

This part of the procedure shows how to use materials that will reinforce what your student has just read. Later, you will learn how to create independent reading activities to further enhance his/her word recognition, vocabulary, comprehension and fluency.

Segment II:

The Failure Free Reading Methodology Sample Lessons

Understanding the Reading Process

Failure Free Reading is based on thirty years of research and development. It is specifically designed to bridge the gap between theory and the need for practical classroom-tested materials and methods. The primary purpose of The Failure Free Reading Methodology is to provide a basic understanding of the reading process to students with pronounced reading difficulty.

Imagine building a house. The plans have been designed and approved. The contractor has been hired. The land has been bought and cleared. The material has arrived. Imagine also that on the first day of construction the blueprints get lost. The contractor assures you that although his men have never seen the blueprint, he will be able to get across his idea. His men are artisans. He assures you not to worry. He can build the house anyway.

Would you build the house? I bet you wouldn't. Why? Because you know, even the most talented artisans cannot build what they cannot see.

Learning to read is like using the blueprints of a house. The teacher is the contractor and the students are his or her workers. Without an adequate understanding of the overall plan or process, few, if any, of the individual pieces (such as letters and words) will make much sense—regardless of the individual's ability. Students need to have a guide, a reading blueprint. The Failure Free Reading Methodology gives non-readers this reading blueprint.

Failure Free Reading gives non-readers an opportunity to immediately experience the reading process. All students, regardless of prior reading ability, can be expected to learn to read fluently, with full comprehension, from meaningful, age-appropriate material!

How the Failure Free Reading Methodology Meets Student Needs

The Failure Free Reading Methodology is designed to help you provide a productive reading experience by meeting essential student needs, such as:

- the need to work with age-appropriate materials
- the need to read independently
- the need for a consistent approach
- the need for repetition
- the need to see immediate progress
- the need to develop confidence
- the need to achieve success
- the need to be challenged
- the need to learn at the fastest appropriate rate
- the need to self-correct
- the need to learn by doing

The Role of the Teacher in the Failure Free Reading Program

Teacher attitude and expectations are critical to the success of The Failure Free Reading Methodology. I firmly believe that the teacher's primary role is to give their non-readers an opportunity to directly experience the reading process.

Remember:

If your non-readers can speak, they can read,
If your non-readers can listen, they can read,
If your non-readers can think, they can read,

Provided:

Non-readers are placed in materials that are in the most comprehensible form and instructed by teachers who believe in their capacity to learn.

I have shown you how to provide materials that are in their most comprehensible form. Now, I expect you to present this material in a non-threatening and highly reinforcing environment. You must expect your non-readers to succeed immediately.

Teacher Directions

Let me restate a key point, you must follow the methodology. While it is acceptable to adapt the program to meet specific classroom or tutorial demands, it must be done within limits. Let your students be your guide. If they experience success and show growing confidence, then continue with what you are doing.

Again, the primary goal of Failure Free Reading is to provide a basic understanding of the reading process. You are the key ingredient to this experience. In order for your non-readers to succeed, it is necessary to do two things: trust in their capacity to learn and follow the program.

A Sample Lesson—Primary Level

This is one of the first lessons I developed in the Failure Free Reading Program's primary reading material. It is designed for young students in the very early grade levels. The story's central theme is one almost every child can relate to: *Going to the Park*. Notice how the sentences in the first paragraph in the story build on sentence structure and comprehension.

"I am going to the park."
"I am going to the park with my father."
"I am going to the park with my father and mother."

Everything is written in simple active declarative sentences. There are no personal names or dates. It is also written in the first person narrative (the easiest story format to understand).

In addition, I use the principle of "cognitive chunking." New information is chunked or expanded upon. The sentence expands by adding new pieces of critical information. This also explains why I can use longer than recommended sentence lengths. Everything builds.

Notice also, the heavy use of repetition. The story constantly repeats and builds on what has just been introduced. This concept of repetition and building is clearly shown in lesson two when the next paragraph is introduced.

"I am going to the park."
"I am going to the park with my father."
"I am going to the park with my father and mother."

"We will drive in our car."
"We will drive in our car to the park."
"We will drive in our car to the park in the country."

Look at the logical extension of the story theme. "Cognitive chunking" continues and logic continues. The story continues to build in a highly repetitive format. It ends with a highly comprehensible story that contains all of the previously introduced paragraphs.

I also selected words that were highly transferable. These are coming from the research based EDL graded core vocabulary list. The EDL Core Vocabularies is the most widely used vocabulary list in the United States. In developing the Core Vocabularies, EDL consulted more than 160 sources, including the major basal reading series, a number of widely used spelling lists, and, for the intermediate levels, the findings of the most authoritative studies of usage by pupils and frequency of occurrence in reading material. Because reading level was the major consideration in determining grade placement, basal readers were used as primary sources.

Among the standardized tests developed with the EDL Core Vocabularies are the TABE and FCAT. EDL contains the words students will see in their textbooks and other reading material. It is estimated that when a student learns 300 new words, that student now has the opportunity to read 15,000 additional books.

Is my approach overkill? Yes, for some poor and struggling readers, but absolutely not for non-readers who have tried everything else and are stuck at "square one." Is it boring? Not if it was determined at the start of the lesson that it was "too hard" for them (either instructionally or independently). My research has shown that when non-readers start with very difficult, yet comprehensible stories, repetition is the "mother of learning."

Now, watch as I present the material, using the Failure Free Reading Methodology of: preview, listen, present, read and review.

Preview

"Today we are going to read a story about a person who is going to go
   to the park with his father and mother."

New Words of Particular Interest:

"You are going to be introduced to many words in this story. You
   might know some of the words. If you do, that's just great. If you
   do not know any of these words, do not worry. You will be able to
   read this anyway. Trust me. You are going to do quite well. Just
   relax."

"Let's go over a few of these words. Don't be afraid to tell me that you
   are not sure what some of these words mean. That's what I am
   here for—to help. Remember, it is impossible to read something
   you don't understand—so please ask me to explain any word you
   don't understand."

"Are you ready? Then let's begin! What does the word _____
   mean?" (Park, Father, Mother)

Please ask your student to define each of the words. Always give
examples that are concrete and can be directly related to his/her own experience. For example:

"What is the name of a 'park' in the community you live in?"
"Can you name another 'park' near you?"

Listening

"Please listen as I read the first part of the story aloud."
"I am going to the park."
"I am going to the park with my father."
"I am going to the park with my father and my mother."

Presenting

"Let's spend a few minutes talking about what we have just learned about the story."

Factual

"What was the person going to do?"
"Who was the person going with?"

Inferential Questions

"I am going to ask you some special kinds of questions about the story. These questions are special because the answers were not given to you in the story. You are to give me answers on what you think would make sense. These answers are based upon your opinion—on what you think. You don't have to be afraid of giving me a wrong answer because there are no right or wrong answers. I am only interested in hearing what you think. Just relax and tell me what you think."
"How do you think the person feels about going to the park?"
"How do you think the parents felt?"
"Why do you think the person was going with his parents?"

Leading Questions

"Let's go over what we know about the story."
"The person is going to the _____."
(Pause and see if the student can give you the appropriate answer. If he/she does, give him/her praise!)

"That's right! The person is going to the park. "

(If he/she doesn't give the appropriate answer, give it to him/her.)

"The person is going to the park with his _____."
"That's great! The person is going to go to the park with his father."
"The person is going to the park with his father and _____."
"Fantastic! The person is going to the park with his father and
    mother."

Reading

"It's now time for you to read the story. It is the same or identical to
    what we have talked about. If you want me to read the sentences
    first, I will. If you don't remember a word, I will tell it to you.
    Don't be nervous. Reading is nothing more than thinking about
    what the story is about and trying to guess or anticipate what you
    think is going to come next. Remember, the key is having to make
    the material make sense. You must always stop reading if it does-
    n't make sense. Ask me to help you."
"Are you ready? Watch as I read the first sentence aloud."
"Are you ready to do it alone or would you like to have me read it
    again?"
"Great! Let's hear you read the sentence!"
"That was fantastic! Are you ready for the next sentence?"
"Now it's your turn to read this sentence."
"Excellent! Let's hear you read both sentences."
"That was terrific!"
"Let's continue. Listen as I read the next sentence to you."
"Now it's your turn."
"Way to go! Great reading! Let me hear you read all three sentences."

(Remember, we are trying to build confidence. Help with any word.
Praise often! Exaggerate! Build pride! Let them know that this is quite an
accomplishment to be able to read an entire paragraph by themselves.)

Review

"That was great reading. I am very proud of you."
"Do you think you could read everything we have just gone over
    today?"

(Have your student reread the new material.)

"Fantastic! You are a terrific reader!"

There you have it. It doesn't seem hard, does it? Just remember the following:

1. The purpose of this lesson is to set the tone for all subsequent lessons. Be positive. Help with any word with which he or she might have difficulty. Above all—praise!
2. This is the format you are expected to follow for each lesson. Try to work the sentence repetitions as casually as possible into the discussion. I call this "creative redundancy." How often can you state and restate the same material without going crazy?
3. The number of times the sentences are read is variable. This is based on the ability level of your students. Let their success and attitude be your guide. Most students will pick it up quickly and need fewer repetitions. Our cognitively challenged students or younger students will need much more. Check their eyes and attention span.
4. Have your students read the entire passage in print as often as they like. Tell them words they might forget. Don't get upset when they forget a word in the very next sentence. They need time to assimilate the material. Trust in the learner.
5. Don't respond immediately if they make an error or do not know a word. Give time to see if they can self-correct. Do not, however, turn it into a word attack lesson. This is not the time for that. The lessons have to move fairly quickly. If we stop too often or too long at one part of the passage because they can't recognize a particular word, your student's short-term memory will be exhausted and he/she will break down. He/she will literally forget that they are reading words connected by meaning. He/she will immediately stop reading for meaning and see each word in isolation.
6. The goal is reading for meaning—not word perfect reading. Let them continue if they make minor omissions and/or substitutions that do not change the overall meaning of the story. For example, do correct them if they read, "I am going to the park with my 'farm' and 'moth'," because this makes no sense. They must be taught that reading must make sense!
7. Don't limit your student. While a student should complete at least one reading lesson a session, they are allowed to do more. The

number of lessons a student does during a tutoring session is arbitrary. Just be sure that they are not frustrated.

Remember, you are the professional. You are to make the determination. Just don't make the mistake of giving them too little or slowing them down if they have not mastered the material in a "word perfect" fashion. You need to find the perfect balance where the material is challenging but they can still comprehend it.

8. Non-readers with good language and command of higher cognitive skills probably will not need the material repeated as often. For them, an initial introduction and the repetition built into the story format will be enough.

    Watch your students' eyes and mannerisms for signs of boredom. Ask them how they like the material. Don't be afraid to combine lessons if you think they can do more. Play with it. Be flexible.

9. The toughest part of the repetition is on you—not your students. Frankly, it does get tiresome hearing the same sentences over and over. When this happens, however, try to remember the success your non-readers are having because of it and you. Remember this, if repetition turned people off, we wouldn't have: commercials, radio, the recording industry or any of the other major industries predicated upon the need for repetition.

10. Always show the students the progress they are making. Exaggerate it! Have them count the number of words and sentences they read. Chart their progress. Give praise. Remember, nothing succeeds like success. The more they enjoy reading, the more they will read.

11. Continue to stress the concept of "does it make sense?"

12. Most of your students should be experiencing success from the very first lesson. Some might not. Don't give up. In many cases, this simply means they need more contact with the material. This is especially true of younger students and the developmentally delayed. These students usually need 10—15 times more practice. So relax, trust the methodology and trust your students. They are learning—even if they might not show it yet. Don't get frustrated. Continue to be patient. It just takes time. Input precedes output.

13. Make word cards for each sentence. Scramble them up and have the students put them in the correct order. Make sentence strips if individual words are too hard. Have your students put the sentence strips in the correct order.

14. Continue to praise constantly.

15. Provide assistance as often as possible.

16. Smile. Relax. Believe in your students. They are learning. They are improving. Wait. Don't be discouraged. Everyone will improve.
17. Don't be upset if some are still having difficulty. Ask them if they would like more practice and assistance. Ask them if there is a literate adult at home who can assist them. Let them take it home and read it silently. Have them write down the words they don't know.
18. Remember to let them try to self-correct. Ask them to read past the word that stumped them. Remind them that the word must make sense within the sentence. Draw their attention to the word by tapping on it or pointing to it. Ask them to look at the word one more time. Research has shown that many students can self-correct when the mistaken word is drawn to their attention a second time.

A Sample Lesson—Secondary or Adult

Before we begin let's state again the most critical thing to remember: reading is relating! If adolescent or adult students don't have enough contact with the print, or meet complex sentence structures, or can't understand the story content, they won't have a successful experience. The key is relating. The Failure Free Reading Methodology instructional procedure insures they will relate. This is where teaching comes into play. How they do is up to your choice of reading material (Step One) and your ability to follow the Failure Free Reading Methodology (Step Two).

Now let us look how I use the Failure Free Reading Methodology with older non-readers. I developed this passage for adolescent non-readers. The passage was developed using a fifth grade word list. I wanted to put these key words into a meaningful story. The theme of explorers came into my mind. Watch as I show you how to teach this very sophisticated—yet highly comprehensible passage.

Preview

"In this part of the story the person talks about how different the explorers acted with their troops."

New Words of Particular Interest:

"You are going to be introduced to many words in this story. You might know some of the words. If you do, that is just great, but if you don't know any of these words, do not worry. You will be able to read this anyway. Trust me. You are going to do quite well. Just relax. Let's go over a few of these words. Don't be afraid to tell me that you are not sure what some of these words mean. That's why I am here—to help. Remember, it is impossible to read something you don't understand—so please ask me to explain any word you don't understand. Are you ready? Then let's begin!

What does the word (phrase) mean?

New words: explorers, slaves, accuse, remark, murmur, glimpse, gloom, discontent, reflect, inquire, slash, whine."

As you can see, there are quite a few words to be introduced. This is why language is so important. You must build on their base. Explain the critical vocabulary in terms they can understand.

For example:

"Have you ever been in a situation when someone tried to blame you for something? This is what "accuse" means. Accuse means to blame. In our story, you will discover that many of the explorers would blame their troops for many different things. In other words, they would blame or "accuse" them for everything. So what does "accuse" mean? That's right, it means to blame."

"Tell me something. Tell me about anything. Great. You have just given me a 'remark.' A remark is a statement. Anything you say aloud is a remark. 'I love school,' 'I hate green beans,' and 'I want to go to sleep,' are all remarks. Remarks can be good or bad or about anything."

Listening

"Please listen as I read a passage that discusses explorers. Let's listen as the person writing the passage describes how explorers were treated and how they treated their troops.

'I was also amazed at how different each explorer was to the troops they led. Some explorers were very popular while other explorers were hated and acted like monsters. I was horrified at how some explorers treated their troops like slaves. Many witnesses talked about how terrified these troops were. These explorers demanded everything from their troops and would accuse them of being traitors if they made even the slightest remark or murmur or glimpse of gloom and discontent. No one was allowed to reflect or inquire about where they were going. Explorers would slash them with weapons. Explorers would not allow any of their troops to whine about their condition and would leave them with no transportation to die if they came down with a sickness.' "

Presenting

Questioning

Factual:

> "How did the explorers treat their troops?"
> "What would explorers slash their troops with?"
> "What would happen if troops became sick?"

Inferential:

> "Why do you think some explorers were so cruel to their troops?"
> "Why do you think some explorers acted like monsters?"
> "What does the phrase slightest remark or murmur or glimpse of gloom and discontent mean?"
> "Why do you think some troops might want to reflect or inquire about where they were going?"
> "What does the phrase 'whine about their condition' mean?"

Leading:

> "Let's go over what we have just learned about this part of the story."
> "I was also amazed at how different each explorer was to the troops they led. Some explorers were very popular while other explorers were hated and acted like _____." (MONSTERS)
> "Great! I was also amazed at how different each explorer was to the troops they led. Some explorers were very popular while other explorers were hated and acted like monsters."

"I was horrified at how some explorers treated their troops like slaves. Many witnesses talked about how _____ these troops were." (TERRIFIED)

"That's right! I was horrified at how some explorers treated their troops like slaves. Many witnesses talked about how terrified these troops were."

"These explorers demanded everything from their troops and would accuse them of being traitors if they made even the slightest remark or murmur or glimpse of gloom and discontent. No one was allowed to reflect or inquire about where they were going. Explorers would slash them with _____." (WEAPONS)

"You are correct! These explorers demanded everything from their troops and would accuse them of being traitors if they made even the slightest remark or murmur or glimpse of gloom and discontent. No one was allowed to reflect or inquire about where they were going. Explorers would slash them with weapons."

"Explorers would not allow any of their troops to whine about their condition and would leave them with no transportation to die if they came down with a _____." (SICKNESS)

"Great! Explorers would not allow any of their troops to whine about their condition and would leave them with no transportation to die if they came down with a sickness." Does this make sense to you?

Reading

"It is now time again for you to read the story. The story is identical to what we have talked about. If you want me to read the sentences first, I will. If you don't remember a word, I will tell it to you.

Don't be nervous. Reading is nothing more than thinking about what the story is saying and trying to guess or anticipate what you think is going to come next. Remember, the key is making the material make sense. Stop reading if it doesn't make sense, ask me to help you."

Repeated Readings

"Are you ready? Watch as I read the first three sentences aloud." (READ ALOUD.)

"Are you ready to do it alone or would you like to have me read it again?"

"Great! Let's hear you read these sentences!"

"That was fantastic! Are you ready for the next three sentences?" (READ THE NEXT SENTENCE.)

"Now it's your turn to read these sentences."

"That was fantastic! Are you ready for the last two sentences?'" (READ THE NEXT SENTENCE.)

"Now it's your turn to read these sentences."

"Excellent! Let's hear you read all of the sentences."

"That was terrific!"

Remember, we are trying to build confidence. Help with any word. Praise often! Exaggerate! Build Pride! Let them know that this is quite an accomplishment to be able to read this by themselves.

Review

"That was great reading. I am very proud of you."

"Do you think you could read everything we have just gone over so far?"

(Have the student reread the material)

"Fantastic! That was great reading!"

Notes to the Instructor

This is a huge lesson. The vocabulary is quite sophisticated. Remember to explain in terms they can understand. Use concrete examples. Make it relevant. It will take time to explain. You might consider breaking it into two parts. Watch their eyes. Build on their base. Question intensely.

Reinforcement Activities

"Practice makes perfect." Sounds trite, doesn't it? Well it isn't. The more practice your students get with this material, the better. The following is an example of how you can turn what they have just read into reinforcement activities. Watch as we turn the new content about explorers into a lesson on "following directions" and "filling in the blanks."

"Please listen as I read the first part of our passage aloud."

"I was also amazed at how different each explorer was to the troops they led. Some explorers were very popular while other explorers were hated and acted like monsters. I was horrified at how some explorers treated their troops like slaves. Many witnesses talked about how terrified these troops were. These explorers demanded everything from their troops and would accuse them of being traitors if they made even the slightest remark or murmur or glimpse of gloom and discontent."

Take the first sentence in this passage and number it and the other sentence in the paragraph. Write each numbered sentence down on a sheet of paper. Do this twice. The first group will be for the following direction activities. The second will be for filling in the blanks.

Look at how we converted the explorer passage into these two formats. Read the directions that follow. Let these notes and directions serve as your model for future activity sheets.

Remember to:

1. Demonstrate
2. Explain
3. Discuss
4. Self-correct

Sample Reinforcement Activities

"The Explorers"

1. I was also amazed at how different each explorer was to the troops they led.
2. Some explorers were very popular while others were hated and acted like monsters.

3. I was horrified at how some explorers treated their troops like slaves.
4. Many witnesses talked about how terrified these troops were.
5. These explorers demanded everything from their troops.

Directions to Your Student:

"Let's do the first sentence together."

"I will always read the directions to you."

"You can always ask me any questions or have the directions repeated as often as you like."

Read sentence #1.

"What was the person amazed at? Underline the word or words that tell what the person was amazed at."

"Watch as I underline my answer."

"What was the person amazed at?"

"That's right, the person was 'amazed at how different each explorer was to the troops they led.' "

Demonstrate: "Watch as I underline the words, 'at how different each explorer was to the troops they led.'"

Explain: "Notice how I underlined only the words, 'at how different each explorer was to the troops they led,' and no more."

Discuss: "Why do you think I only underlined those particular words? That's right! I only underlined, 'at how different each explorer was to the troops they led,' because they were the only words I needed to answer the question."

Self-correct: "How did you do?"

"It's all right if your answers do not match mine exactly today. Try to do so in the future. The purpose of this lesson is to help you recognize individual words and phrases. Do not underline just any word or more words than you need. Underline only what you will need to answer the question. Is this clear? Are there any questions?"

2. Read sentence #2.

   "How did some of the explorers act? Underline the word or words that tell how some of the explorers acted."

3. Read sentence #3.

   "What horrified the person? Underline the word or words that tell what horrified the person."

4. Read sentence #4.

   "What does the witnesses talk about? Underline the word or words that tell what the witnesses talked about."

5. Read sentence #5.

   "What did the explorers demand? Underline the word or words that tell what the explorers demanded."

Notes to Remember for Anyone Who is Teaching a Student How to Read:

1. Modeling is very important. Repeat the modeling steps of Demonstration, Explanation, Discussion, and Self-correction as often as is needed. Talk through these stages so your student can hear and see how you would have selected your answer.
2. Allow your students to self-correct and change answers. Self-correction is critical to the learning process. Many times we think a student can't self correct when he/she can actually correct if it's brought to his/her attention.
3. Again, don't give them the correct answer without first giving them an opportunity to self-correct. Don't let this take long. Tapping the mistaken word with a pencil is a quick way to make sure they are staying on task. Or quickly saying, "Why don't you look at that word again," is also valuable. Don't make this an elaborate procedure. If they can't correct immediately, tell them the word and move on. This is not the time for word attack. Self-correcting and word-attack are not the same.

4. Self-correcting might be hard at first. Be patient. Talk it out. Relax and don't push it. It will come in time.

5. Stop the exercise if it becomes too frustrating. You can always come back to it. Remember, the purpose of these activities is to build confidence and self-worth. They are not to be graded. Write great things on the paper. Make your student feel good. Build pride!

Directions on How to Introduce Silent Reading Fill in the Blank Activities

Now watch as I create "filling in the blank" activities. These are often called "cloze" activities. Cloze activities promote reading comprehension. You'll see they are not very hard to create. I'll use our explorer passage as our example,

Directions to Your Student:

"The next part of the page you are about to do contains sentences from your story. None of the sentences are complete. A key word or phrase is missing. You must choose a word from the three choices listed below the sentence. Let's look at the first sentence."

1. I was also _____at how different each explorer was to the troops they led.
   a. parent's   b. amazed   c. get

"Here is a hint to help you complete the sentences: You can tell if you have the correct word by reading the sentence to yourself after you have chosen a word."
"You are correct if the sentence makes sense. You will need to find another word if the sentence does not make sense."
"Look at the first sentence. It says, 'I was also _____ (PAUSE) at how different each explorer was to the troops they led.' " The word "blank" confuses many students. Never say "blank." Merely pause for a second and continue reading.
"Look at the three choices below the sentence. The three choices are: 'parent's,' 'amazed,' and 'get.' "
Check to see if your students are at the correct part of the page.

"I am going to pick one of the choices. I am going to pick 'parent's.'
Let's see if 'parent's' is a good choice."

"Listen as I read the sentence: Does the sentence—'I was also parent's
at how different each explorer was to the troops they led'—make
sense? No, it does not! Reading must always make sense. This
sentence does not have any sense or meaning when I use the word
'parent's.' I have to find a better choice."

"What word do you think we could select from our choices? Would
you select 'amazed' or 'get' ?"

"That's right 'amazed' is our best choice because amazed makes the
most sense. Try to finish the rest of the sentences by yourself. I
will help you with any words you do not know."

"Circle your choice and remember; you should always check your
answers by reading the complete sentence to see if it makes
sense."

Notes

See how easy this is to create the activities? Always talk them through it
like I just did. You can do this. It's easy. No sweat. It just takes time.

Points to Remember

1. The purpose of the first lesson is to set the tone for all subsequent
   fill in the blank lessons. Be positive. Help them with any word
   with which they might have difficulty. Above all: praise!
2. Remember the importance of modeling. Repeat the modeling
   steps of Demonstration, Explanation, Discussion, and Self-correction as often as is needed. Talk through these stages so your
   student can hear and see how you would select an answer.
3. Stop the exercise if it becomes too frustrating. You can always
   come back to it. Remember, the purpose of these sessions is to
   build confidence and self-worth. Make your student feel good.
   Build pride!
4. Check to see that your students understand this concept of "making sense." I have found reading each choice in the sentence aloud
   and voicing the reasons why I would not select that choice helps.
5. Please remember to monitor your students' answers especially
   during the first lessons. Help them immediately if they make a

mistake. Try to have it appear, however, that they are self-correcting the material. Treat the corrected response as a first time response. Remember the purpose is to instill confidence.

6. Please remember to praise your students' answers. Remember this can be very hard for non-readers. And do not be upset if your students need more practice and assistance. You set the pace.

Final Advice

There you have it. That is the Failure Free Reading Methodology and reading approach in a nutshell. Now it doesn't seem hard, does it? Don't be anxious. You have all the skills. All you need is to try it out.

I hope through reading this book you have gained a better understanding about the programs that are available to non-readers and what may be right for your non-reader. I hope that you understand that what may be right for one student is never right for every single student that follows. No one student is the same and we can't expect everyone to fit the same mold.

The current education system may have its flaws and it certainly does have its share of stubborn people in it. However, we are lucky and should be thankful that for all the fuss and controversy; people truly are trying to do right by their students. If we didn't care about the ability to read, there wouldn't be any controversy.

So remember to do your homework and be open-minded. Never underestimate the impact of positive thinking and powerful motivation. There is no need to leave any student behind any more just because they don't fit into the majority. There is a solution and an answer, there are too many students growing up in a world that has told them nothing but "no," and has labeled them as "slow," and an "underachiever." We have to expect more from all students—especially non-readers and they must expect more from themselves. They have the ability to read, to learn, and to succeed.

Please read the last section of the book: Common Questions. Then get ready to give the gift of reading to someone who needs your help. Together we can make a huge difference in the lives of those who need our help the most.

Appendix A:

Commonly Asked Questions from Parents and Educators

What is the main purpose behind The Failure Free Reading Methodology?

The primary purpose of Failure Free Reading is to give parents, teachers, and other interested individuals the chance to save lives and reinstate dignity, pride and self respect to our non-readers by proving to them that they can read faster, comprehend higher and do much more. Failure Free Reading gives non-readers the opportunity to experience immediately what it feels like to read fluently, with full comprehension, from age-appropriate material regardless of their prior reading ability.

What makes The Failure Free Reading Methodology so different?

Speed is what sets Failure Free Reading apart from other reading programs. All too often, non-readers are placed in reading intervention programs that are too slow. Most require between 40 to 100 hours of intensive instruction before non-readers can experience what it feels like to read somewhat fluently with some comprehension from anything that even slightly comes close to grade level. It's hard to believe, but most of the "well known" intervention programs actually require students to receive treatment for periods of one to three years! I guess this might be fine if the program is somewhat appropriate, but what happens when it is not? What happens when students are misplaced and required to stay in the wrong treatment for an extensive period, simply because there was no quick measurement of response to treatment? What should we say to these students or their parents when all they experienced is nothing more than two and three more years of additional failure?

Sadly, under our nation's current education system most of the responsibility for success lies on the non-readers' shoulders. Students are labeled, and excuses are made for program failure. Program developers, in giving reasons why their program is showing only minimal growth for some students, are always quick to point the blame to others. "The teachers didn't follow the program exactly as we asked." "We started too late in the year." "The student isn't motivated." Or the worse excuse of all: "The student just needs a little more time."

Ultimately, a "little more time" turns from months into years. The student is then retained or drops out of school or is enrolled in special education and then turns into a "special ed lifer." This is a national tragedy. Educators and researchers can't have it both ways. They can't say we need to use the "medical model" as our treatment standard and then only offer mid to long-term treatment procedures. Many students are in cardiac arrest. They are in the emergency room on the table, in pronounced reading failure. They can't wait mid to long-term. They need immediate life saving help. Fortunately, Failure Free Reading provides this.

Failure Free Reading specializes in "educational triage." Failure Free Reading is not just designed for mid or long-term treatment. Failure Free Reading is out in the tents, on the battlefield, saving the lives of the neediest victims of the "reading wars." Failure Free Reading is specifically designed to stop immediately the bleeding so the patient will not slowly bleed to death out in the field. I know this is hard to believe but 95% of non-readers demonstrate significant reading improvement within the first 30 minutes of the Failure Free Reading treatment. This is the beauty of the program. Decision makers don't have to wait weeks, months or years to know if the treatment is appropriate; they'll know within hours!

What do you mean by "special ed lifers"?

I would like to share with you what I call special education's "dirty little secret." I know this secret because, as a former school psychologist, special education director, special education teacher and university professor, I've experienced this secret first hand. I first discovered it as a special education teacher over thirty years ago. The secret is as strong today as it was thirty years before. When it comes to students who have very hard-core reading difficulties, special education does not know what to do with them, anymore than regular education does. That's right, after an elaborate student identification and special education labeling process, the vast majority of these newly labeled special education students enter special education, stay in special education, and fall further and further behind because of special education. Why? Because all they are receiving are variations on the exact same theme.

For example, let us say you have a non-reader who is a product of a phonics based regular education reading program. The student is "phonetically deaf" and just failing miserably in the classroom. This student is with a caring teacher who has provided remedial help. They go over the sounds, drills and phonetic rules over and over and over. Still, the student shows no growth. The teacher refers the student for special education.

The special education child study team does identify a huge gap in achievement. The student is classified, an individualized education plan is written, and the student is put into a special education class run by one of their best teachers who has been specially trained in one of the best nationally known remedial methods. Sadly, this student is doomed. The dye is cast and his/her fate is sealed. This student has a ninety-nine percent chance of becoming a "special ed lifer." Why? You guessed it. The "best method" is intensive instruction in phonics. That's right. A student who failed miserably in a phonics-based classroom is now going to get more phonics. This doesn't make sense. It is a lot like a physician giving a diabetic more sugar in order to treat sugar intolerance.

What is the treatment for "special ed lifers?"

The best treatment is common sense. Special education should not provide more of the same solution for our non-readers. Non-readers are failing because they are different. They need viable reading alternatives that allow them to capitalize on their strengths while minimizing their weaknesses. Failure Free Reading does this. It allows students with a "tin ear for sounds" to learn to read without phonics. It also allows students with limited experiences and language skills to learn to read as well.

Is "whole language" the logical educational alternative for "phonetically deaf" students?

Absolutely not! Let me make this clear. For non-readers, the opposite of phonics is not whole language. There are just as many problems with "whole language" for non-readers as there are with phonics. Let me explain. Non-readers have three characteristics that set them apart. The first is that they can be "phonetically deaf." Obviously, when this occurs, they need an alternative to phonics-based programs. However, they can also have other characteristics as well, such as being "environmentally denied" and/or "language deprived." For these students, whole language is just as hard as phonics. Why? Because they don't have the necessary background experiences to relate to the many different story themes and/or they don't have the language base to understand all the new terms and idiomatic expressions found in traditional whole language stories.

Just like phonics, whole language is simply too complex for non-readers. Non-readers need to be initially placed in a program that controls for the simultaneous utilization of repetition, sentence structure and story content.

Why should reading material be so repetitious?

The average student needs to see a word somewhere between 25 to 45 times before he or she can independently recognize the word. Researchers have found non-readers need much more contact than this.

Hargis found in a study of students with severe reading difficulties that the single most important criteria for word recognition was not word attack skills (phonics), or I.Q. or background. It was repetition. Poor readers in his study needed to see words an average of 76 times or more before they could recognize each word in isolation for three consecutive times. It didn't make any difference whether the words were phonetically regular or not.

Traditional remedial methodologies do not provide for this much repetition. Many words are introduced too quickly in many stories and seen only once or twice. This is not enough for non-readers. Non-readers need to be placed in highly redundant material if they are to succeed with more challenging material. When they are placed in more challenging material, non-readers actually crave the repetition. Repetition is a soothing tonic. In this situation, repetition can be the mother of all learning.

Why aren't non-readers bored by Failure Free Reading's redundancy? Isn't this just "drill and kill?"

No, they are not bored and Failure Free Reading is not "drill and kill." Non-readers are not bored when placed in material that comes closest to their real grade level and in a methodology that stresses multiple exposures in multiple contexts. Failure Free Reading does both.

The Failure Free Reading's Diagnostic Placement Test is designed to enter non-readers at their most challenging level. Students are entered only when they test or say that this material is "too hard, I can't do this." I have found that when students are placed at their "too hard" level, repetition is the not boring but the mother of learning. Failure Free Reading then replaces "drill and kill" by presenting its material in as many different ways as possible. Non-readers will see it, hear it, say it, write it, and read it. This is the notion of multiple exposures in multiple contexts. If the student is bored, then they are placed at the wrong level. The material must balance between being challenging and still being able to be fully comprehended by the student.

What do you mean by "creative redundancy?"

Creative redundancy is a process in which you try to say the same thing in as many different ways as possible. Try to repeat and reemphasize a word in a casual and comfortable manner. Slip it into the conversation. Do not sound like a meaningless robot who merely says the same thing repeatedly without meaning and expression. Creative redundancy is the opposite of "drill and kill."

Why is sentence structure important?

Sentence structure is directly related to comprehension. Many non-readers come from homes in which Standard English is not the spoken language. They lack an intuitive understanding of the rules of grammar. Usually this can be seen in a non-reader's writing. The words are unusually unconnected and make little or no sense. Unfortunately, controlling for sentence structure is overlooked in reading intervention programs. Complex sentences, inverted phrases, dependent clauses, and incomplete sentences, all of which affect the non-reader's ability to have a successful reading experience, are used from the very first stories. Failure Free Reading is one of the first, if not the only, reading program to control for sentence structure. Failure Free Reading stories are written in the easiest and most predictable sentence structures. Most are simple declarative sentences. Inverted phrases, dependent clauses, personal names, dates, and complex sentences have all been controlled for in the Failure Free Reading material.

Why is story content important?

Reading is gaining meaning from the printed page. Many non-readers are unable to read for meaning because they can't relate to the story. This is especially true for limited English language learners. Too much reading material requires that students have experiential prerequisites in order to be successful. In other words, these students must know something about the story's language, phrases, names or theme before they are asked to read it for meaning. The less they know prior to reading it, the more they are going to fail as they read it.

Figurative speech, multiple-words and story content all impact on reading ability. Many students get confused by words that have many different meanings. They are not comfortable hearing idioms and figurative speech. They lack the necessary experiences to relate to the story's central theme.

As is the case with sentence structure, Failure Free Reading is one of the first, if not the only, reading program to control for story content. Failure Free Reading stories do not have uncommon names, dates and places. Figurative speech and idiomatic expression is kept to a minimum. When the stories become more complex, they are carefully pre-taught before the students are ever exposed to them in print. This pre-teaching is one of the keys to Failure Free Reading's success.

Who can I use Failure Free Reading with?

Failure Free Reading can be used with students who: are failing, do not have a "good ear" for sounds, need a global approach, need an immediate confidence builder, need to work on their "sight" vocabulary, or have a limited English background.

Failure Free Reading is particularly strong with non-readers in the No Child Left Behind reading subgroups: limited English, special education, minority, and low income. In special education, Failure Free Reading works very well with severely Learning Disabled, Mild and Moderate Mentally Retarded as well as Autistic, Emotionally Disturbed, Speech and Language and Deaf students.

Do you have any research to substantiate your claims?

Absolutely. Failure Free Reading is supported by over thirty years of quantitative and qualitative research. This research ranges from seven published articles in national and international reading research journals to over 80 different studies involving over 8,000 students of all ages and classifications. All of our studies have shown significant and, in most cases, dramatic increases in reading growth and ability. We have also been asked to help schools reduced the number of special education placements.

Perhaps the two most impressive gains (in addition to significant growth in reading comprehension, fluency and word recognition) are in the self-concept and attitude exhibited by the students involved in the Failure Free Reading program. Teachers and parents continually mention students and children who are smiling more and telling them how much better they feel about themselves.

How does Failure Free Reading fit into the concept of learning styles?

The Failure Free Reading Methodology blends very well with the concept of learning styles. This program is excellent for the student with a global learning style—a student who needs a basic understanding of the overall reading process. It is also excellent for "visual learners"—students who have a good visual memory and/or students who have weakness in both "auditory" and "visual" areas.

What is the most important aspect of The Failure Free Reading Methodology from the standpoint of teachers, parents and students?

Failure Free Reading takes the blame off teachers, students and parents. Too often, it is assumed that if students cannot read it is because they do not want to, or they were poorly taught, or they came from homes where the parents did not care. Teachers tend to blame the students and parents for not trying. Parents tend to blame the teachers for not teaching. Why? Because they're all frustrated and don't know who else to blame.

This is wrong. The real culprit is the material and the method. The Failure Free Reading Methodology is designed to attack the problems contained within the stories being used and the way they are being presented to non-readers.

What do you mean by material and method?

As I have mentioned, until recently most reading programs fell into one of two broad classifications known as the "bottom-up" or the "top-down" models. The bottom-up model views the reading process as a series of discrete stages. Proponents believe reading must first concentrate on the perception of letters and words. In other words, students are expected to master their letters and letter sounds before they can be placed into more meaningful reading material.

Advocates of the top-down model believe reading is more than letter and word identification. They see reading as a higher-level cognitive process, which requires the successful interaction between the reader and the printed material. Top-down theorists believe readers do not read letter by letter or word by word because it impedes comprehension.

So who's right? The answer is both. Students do need to know how to recognize individual words and letters. They also need to work in meaningful and age-appropriate reading materials from the very start. In other words, the fluent reader must be able to compute many different kinds of information in a relatively short period, functionally in parallel.

Keith E. Stanovich (1980), noted Canadian reading researcher, was one of the first to mention a compensatory component to such a model. According to this, readers with a weakness in one area will use information from another to compensate. In other words, students with poor word recognition skills will use context to figure the word out if given a chance and if placed in a context that is meaningful, well written, and within their current experience.

Unfortunately, remedial and traditional reading methods never give students the opportunity to demonstrate a reading strength in sight words or the use of contextual clues because they continue to use instructional stories that are not meaningful, redundant or written in a basic sentence structure.

As Charles H. Hargis, a national expert on the importance of providing appropriate curricular materials to students with pronounced reading problems stated in his book, *Teaching Reading to Handicapped Children*, "Teachers often complain about inconsistent responses from students who have severe reading problems. 'They seem to know the words one day but not the next.' This observation reflects a problem of children not introduced to words in meaningful context with sufficient repetition and who have not, as yet, been able to do any meaningful reading—often after years in school, they fall into this predicament because there are no published materials with sufficient controls to permit meaningful activities."

My daughter has been diagnosed as dyslexic. Does your program work for dyslexics or do I need to go to a trained specialist?

The issue of dyslexia is still very controversial. Some even question its existence. They prefer to use the term learning disabled. This is generally true if they are associated with schools. Others, however, strongly disagree with this. They believe dyslexia is a neurologically based condition. This is generally true if they are associated with hospitals and physicians.

Research indicates that there are at least three different types of dyslexic conditions. There is the audio phonological dyslexic, the visual-spatial dyslexic and the mixed dyslexic. The audio phonological dyslexic, which is the most prevalent, has a poor ear for sounds and does not learn well through a phonetic or skills based approach. The visual-spatial dyslexic experiences difficulty organizing symbols in space and time. They usually have pronounced reversals and unusual spelling patterns. The mixed dyslexic, which is a combination of both, is smallest in number and the most difficult to treat.

Failure Free Reading has been shown to be very effective with all three types, especially the mixed dyslexic, because it allows him/her to compensate for a weakness in one area and capitalize on the strengths he/she brings to the task.

My daughter is eight years old and still writes her numbers and letters backwards. She has been referred at her school for special testing. Does she really see backwards?

As I mentioned earlier, your child is not "seeing backwards." There is no neurological evidence to substantiate the claim that your child "sees backwards." This claim is actually being inferred based on her performance in school and on isolated tests, many of which can actually cause reversals.

How can these tests and tasks cause the reversals? Because they are given to your child out of context. This denies your child the opportunity to use meaning or context as a measuring tool. Confused? Don't be.

It is very easy to read, "saw" for "was" or "no" for "on" when presented with these words in isolation. It is next to impossible to reverse or confuse these words in a meaningful context. Why? Because the meaning or context would prevent it.

It just doesn't make sense to reverse words. No one, for example, young or old, would substitute the word "was" for the word "saw" in the following sentence: "I saw my dog eat a bone." Why? Because to do so would make absolutely no sense. What does "I was my dog eat a bone" mean? Nothing!

Who would ever think of reading "I placed the book no the table by the chair." For "I placed the book on the table by the chair." It just doesn't make sense to reverse given the context.

If your child does reverse while reading aloud, you can bet that there is something within the material and not within her that is causing it to happen. In most cases, you'll probably find that the paragraph or sentence uses poor sentence structure or has unusual vocabulary or story theme. She can't relate to something in the material. The context is no longer comprehensible. This lack of comprehensibility is forcing her to see the words in isolation without the benefit of a meaningful context.

Finally, writing isolated words and letters backwards is still very age-appropriate for an eight year old. This has more to do with a confusion of left and right than it does with her "seeing backwards." Research indicates that most children won't acquire mastery of right and left until they are between 6-8 years old. You're child who is eight is still in the average range.

My son is in the first grade and is not doing very well in reading. His teacher recommends keeping him back. She is a very respected teacher in the community and has over 20 years experience. Should I follow her advice?

I strongly advise against retention under any circumstances. Retention doesn't work. The risks of succeeding are greatly outweighed by the chances of failure. The research is clear. Students who are retained are 2.6 times more likely to drop out of school. I have seen case upon case of what happens when well-intentioned professionals and parents decided it is in the child's best interest to hold them back, and it fails.

In Shane R. Jimerson's article, *Meta-analysis of grade retention research: Implications for practice in the 21st century*, he states that, "Although grade retention is widely practiced, it does not help children to 'catch up.' Retained children may appear to do better in the short-term, but they are at much greater risk for future failure than their equally achieving, non-retained peers" (p. 84). A recent review of the association between grade retention and dropping out of high school demonstrates that children retained during elementary school are at an increased risk of dropping out of high school (Jimerson, Anderson, & Whipple, 2001). One study reported that up to 78% of dropouts were retained at least once (Tuck, 1989); others suggest that grade retention increases the risk of dropping out between 20% and 50% (Bachman, Green, & Wirtanen, 1971; Jimerson, 1999). It has been reported that retained students are 2 to 11 times more likely to drop out (Cairns, Cairns, & Neckerman, 1989; Ensminger & Slusarick, 1992; Grissom & Shepard, 1989; Roderick, 1994, 1995). Grade retention has been identified as the single most powerful predictor of dropping out (Rumberger, 1995). Considering assorted evidence suggesting short-term gains, altering of achievement/behavioral trajectories, and mixed achievement and adjustment outcomes correlated with grade retention, the striking association of grade retention and dropping out of high school has led to the statement "we've won the battle but lost the war," in reference to the long-term outcomes of grade retention (Dawson, 1998, p. 21). Educational professionals, researchers, and politicians reviewing the efficacy of grade retention on academic success would benefit from awareness of the literature addressing the association between grade retention and dropping out. (Jimerson)

I couldn't agree more with Jimerson's position as noted in the following personal story. I once met a boy playing at the playground in our neighborhood. He was a nice, older boy who was playing with my two children on the seesaw. He asked my two children what grades they were in and then proceeded to tell me very sadly that he was nine years old and in the 2nd grade. "I failed the easiest grade—kindergarten," he said. "I bet you never heard of somebody failing kindergarten!"

This is an example of shame. This boy has placed the mark of a failure on himself and his self-image reflects it. Once a child has labeled himself or herself as a failure it is so difficult to change this image to a positive one.

Nothing is more important than instilling dignity and respect among our children and youth. Retention robs them of this. No matter what a parent or a teacher does to try to prevent it, it can't be stopped. Why? Because the child will place it on itself regardless of what is done to prevent it.

I once did a study where I interviewed over 50 school-aged students attending a summer remedial program at the University of South Carolina. I was in charge of the program and responsible for overseeing the graduate level students who were to work with these students. The students ranged in age from first grade to high school. The fifty students I interviewed had all been held back at least once in school.

The most interesting result is that all of them were still very far behind academically. None of these students had caught up. Most were much older than their classmates and not doing very well socially in school. It didn't work for them and it won't work for you, especially when you can stop a student's reading failure through our program, quickly, easily, painlessly.

What is the best thing I can do to improve my child's reading at home?

Take every opportunity to expand and develop your child's vocabulary and language skills. Turn each and every reading lesson into a language lesson. Talk about new words and strange phrases. Discuss and expand every chance you get. Vocabulary is critical for future success. The more words your child comes into contact with, the more he/she will be able recognize them in print.

Does your program work for preschoolers?

Yes. It works beautifully for those preschoolers who are ready to experience what reading feels like fluently with full comprehension. It also gives them a basic understanding of the reading process.

Is the phonics approach a bad approach?

It's not bad. It's just that by itself, it's too limiting. It's too restrictive. Too many words are phonetically irregular. In addition, it is too demeaning for adolescents and adults to use. It takes too long for them to have an actual reading experience.

What is the "look say" approach?

"Look say" is just another name for sight word reading. Students learn to recognize the words by sight. In the simplest of all terms: they "look" at the word and then they "say" the word. They do not sound the words out. They tap into the brain's non-phonic word recognition route. Of course, we know that this not possible unless the student has had adequate contact which each of these words within a very meaningful context and that all instruction insures the student knows what the words mean after automatic word recognition occurs.

What do you mean when you say phonics and "look say" can be dangerous?

The danger is if the wrong approach is used with the wrong student. Both methods work for most. Unfortunately, they don't work for all. Forget what you hear about one approach being better than the other; it simply is not true. As we have seen, students can fail with either approach.

Generally speaking, just as many students fail with phonics as they do in "look say." The number appears to be approximately 30% in regular education and up to 50% for special education. However, while the failure rate is the same, the students are different.

In the forties, fifties and sixties, students with poor visual memory did not do well with "look say." In the eighties and nineties students those with poor phonetic skills did not do well with phonics. While I'm not putting either approach down, don't be fooled into thinking that one is significantly better for all students.

If your child is struggling with letters and sounds, try "look say." If they are having difficulty remembering sight words, phonics could be right for them. If he/she is struggling with both, go back and read this book.

What should I do if I feel no one is listening to me at my child's school?

Follow the chain of command. Start with the teacher, move to the principal, and then go to the superintendent. Ask that everything be in writing. Don't be pushy. Just remember that, "the squeaky wheel does get the grease." Ask that your child have an immediate successful reading experience with age-appropriate materials.

Some are saying that all my child is doing is memorizing and not reading from your approach. What about the issue of memorization?

This is a frequently asked question. Yes, they do memorize in the beginning. Quite frankly that's what initial school performance is based on. They have to memorize the phonetic rules and the math rules and the spelling rules and so on.

As they go on, this memorization turns into understanding. They begin to understand what the process is about and become driven by their success.

Why does a child recognize a word in one part of a story and fail to recognize the same word in another part of the story?

For the same reason they reverse. There is something in the material that makes the material meaningless to the reader. It denies them the use of context and forces them to rely exclusively on the graphic information contained in the text. This makes the process more complicated. If they are doing this, then check the complexity of sentence structure, vocabulary and story content.

Why does my child do so well with one story, page or paragraph and then so poorly with the next story, page or paragraph?

For the same reason given in the previous answer. They can't relate to something in the new story, page or paragraph. Again, be sure to check: repetition, sentence structure, vocabulary, and story content.

My child can read but can't do the work sheets in his class. Does this make sense and what should I do?

Yes, it makes great sense. Unfortunately, that's about all that will make sense. You can bet the work sheets won't. Look at the work sheets. Many follow no logic. They amount to what constitutes "busy work." This is why your child needs to have a consistent format.

Keeping students back a year or giving them poor grades because they can't do these foolish work sheets is criminal. It is a classic case of the tail wagging the dog. Don't allow your child to be penalized because some publisher put together a series of isolated and fragmented sheets that make little, if any sense. Remember the notion of basic skills is open to question. There is no rhyme or reason to it. Don't allow your child and you to become victims. If these activities aren't consistent in their format and can't be shown to directly relate to what they are reading in their stories, don't use them. Bring this to your principal's attention. *(Please go to page 2 and read the example in the selection, "Blaming Reading Failure on Motivation," for an example of poor "busy work")*

What do you think about the use of comic books as reading tools for non-readers?

I advise against it for the beginning or struggling non-reader. Comic books are not easy to read. Many have adult themes and stress adult humor. The humor is rich in figurative speech and idiomatic expression. In addition, they usually are very complex in sentence structure. Comics might be good to use at a later date, but not during the initial reading experience.

Tell me again the difference between visual and non-visual information. What is the relationship between visual and non-visual information?

Visual information is contained on the printed page, the print itself. Non-visual information is what the readers bring to the reading. It is based upon their past experiences and their intuitive knowledge of the syntactic and semantic rules which govern our language.

While proficient reading is based upon the successful utilization of both visual and non-visual information, they are not used in equal proportion. An inverse relationship exists between the use of visual and non-visual information. In other words, the more you concentrate on what each letter or word looks like, the less you will be able to concentrate on what they mean.

Consider the following: you have been asked to read two stories. Both stories were written using approximately the same number of words and same level of difficulty as measured by traditional readability formulas. The first is about ancient Mayan customs. The second is a down to earth story about life in your town. Which one would you read faster? Which one would you read with greater clarity? If you are like most, you probably would have said the story about life in your town.

So, why was one story easier to read? The answer lies with the concept of comprehensibility. The more you knew, the more you could anticipate what was on the page. You used your eyes (visual information) merely to confirm your meaningful predictions about the story and the author's purpose (non-visual information). If you were correct (it made sense) you moved on. If you were incorrect (it did not make sense) you went back, corrected your error and then went ahead.

What is comprehensibility?

The average person reads between 250–600 words a minute. Some can even read upwards of 1000–1500 words or more per minute while still maintaining good comprehension. Many would be quite surprised to learn that according to some researchers this commonplace occurrence is a physiological impossibility. It simply can't happen! Yet it does.

The brain is limited to the amount of information it can process at one time. Researchers have cited the brain can process approximately 7—10 bits of information within a three second interval. Given this the brain is limited to the processing of between 140 and 200 bits of information within a 60 second interval (7-10 x twenty three-second intervals). Yet as was previously noted the average person exceeds this by much more. How can this be reconciled?

The answer to this reconciliation lies in the notion of a bit and the concept of comprehensibility. While the brain is limited to the number of individual bits of information it can process within a given time period, it is not limited to the amount of information contained in each bit.

Think of each bit as a container and the brain as a storage shed. The brain can only store seven to ten of these containers during each time interval. The key then is to increase the size of the containers or the amount of information stored in each. And the key to this lies in the concept of comprehensibility.

Many researchers have stated that reading is a "psycho-educational" guessing game. According to this, good readers are not simply passive participants in the reading process. They do not just sit back and let the process unfold. Good readers make things happen. They are active participants in the process.

Good readers are constantly attempting to anticipate what the writer is attempting to say. They do this because of an innate drive to process information in the fastest, most efficient way—to store it quickly into a container and move on to the next one.

Good readers are constantly making predictions about what the author is attempting to say. These predictions, however, are not random guesses. They are based on their previous knowledge of the subject matter (semantics) and their intuitive understanding of what grammatical patterns accompany each other (syntax). Good readers use their eyes simply to confirm their predictions. If correct, they move ahead. If incorrect, they go back, find their mistake and then continue on.

Meaningful context is critical to the prediction process. No student can make meaningful predictions from meaningless stories. All students will fail when the stories they are asked to read are not redundant, poorly written or contain too many uncommon names, dates, places and idioms. These readers are then forced to rely exclusively on visual information and revert to reading letter by letter and word by word, simply because they are denied access to non-visual information found in comprehensible material.

Why do you think it is better to put struggling non-readers into higher grade level material?

Consider the following two examples:

> The man got up early in the morning and took a trip on the early commuter train so he could get to his business in the city on time.
> The man got up early in the morning. Then he took a trip on the early commuter train. So he could get to his business in the city on time.

Which example is easier to read? If you are like most people, you would probably say the first is more comprehensible. Guess what? The second example, which is very choppy and made up of two phrases, is the least comprehensible. Yet, it has the easiest readability level! Why? Because readability formulas only consider the length of the sentence and the size of the words. Meaning or context or sentence structure or comprehensibility is never taken into consideration.

That is why it can be better to put struggling readers into higher grade material right from the start because the sentences, while longer in size are generally better written and more comprehensible. They are less choppy, more complete, and usually make more sense.

How can I prepare my preschooler for the SAT?

By developing your preschooler's language skills. Talk to them. Introduce a new multi-syllable word for the day. Explain the word in a way they can understand. For example: you might want to introduce the word: "Kinesiology." Ask your child if he or she has ever heard of "Kinesiology." Ask them if they can say "Kinesiology." Praise them for anything he/she says in response. Tell them that "Kinesiology" means the study of how people move their bodies. A person who studies or watches how people use their bodies to move is called a "Kinesiologists." For example, "The man went to a Kinesiologist to learn how to teach his son to throw a ball."

The longer the word the better. Don't be afraid if they can't repeat the definition. This is just to have them become familiar with multi-syllable words and phrases at an early age. This will reduce future fear and help them become more aware of sophisticated vocabulary. Read sophisticated stories to them. Talk about these words and stories. Remember: language, language, language.

What are the factors that affect predictability?

Predictability can be increased through familiarity, frequency and context. Predictability is based on the interaction between text, sentence structure and story content.

What is meant by "teaching the basics"?

Your guess is as good as mine when it comes to the definition of the "basics." It appears that while everyone can tell you why we need the basics, very few are in agreement as to what the basics are. So be cautious about programs that stress a return to the "basics." Make sure their definition of basics is appropriate for your child. If it's working, keep it. But if your child is failing, get them what they need.

What do you think about reading failure?

I think reading failure can be wiped off the face of the earth. There is no reason why students have to fail. They are victims. They are victims of an ignorance in which many professionals are more concerned with proving that their particular reading philosophy is better than another.

The days of phonics versus whole language versus basal readers should be laid to rest. They all work. We know it. There is nothing to prove. Now let's get on with developing material for the students who need more.

Appendix B:

30 Ways to Improve Your Student's Reading Ability

Step 1

Forget the Past

All students can learn to read regardless of their prior reading ability. So forget the past. Forget where these students have come from and start looking at where they are going. When we set low expectations, we will achieve low expectations. Past performance is an excuse for poor future performance. All students can read faster, comprehend higher and complete more. If you believe, they will succeed provided they are placed in the most comprehensible instructional materials using a methodology that doesn't accept failure.

Step 2

Become A Gardener

A gardener knows that the chances for a tall plant to grow from a small seed improves when the environment is at its best. This is what the gardener can control for. A gardener can be sure that the soil is rich and well fertilized. A gardener can be sure that the seeds are placed in the best appropriate spot for their individual needs.

The garden must be watered, weeded, and protected. Time is given for optimum growth. Gardeners know that you really can't rush Mother Nature. The plants are not pushed or expected to hurry up. They are not yelled at or left to fend for themselves. They are supported and nurtured every step of the way with the hope that if the gardener has done the job right, the plants will grow. This same principle applies when you are reading with your student.

No one will teach your student how to read. Reading isn't taught. Reading is developed. Just like the seeds in the garden, reading develops best in the right environment. Don't rush the reading process. Never doubt your student's ability to learn. Remember: they have learned how to speak—a much more difficult process—and they will learn how to read! All you have to do is set the right reading conditions.

Step 3

Don't Expect Word Perfect Reading

Don't expect word perfect reading. Most students are not going to read each word perfectly. This is acceptable. In fact, it is a very good sign. We want them to make mistakes. We want them to know that reading is not saying every word right. We want them to know that reading is first and foremost: gaining meaning from the printed page.

Listen to their mistakes. Learn the difference between good mistakes and bad mistakes.

Good mistakes occur when the meaning of the story is not changed. For example, a child who substitutes the word "children" for the word "kids" in the sentence: "The kids are on the playground," has made a good mistake. The meaning has not changed and it shows that the overall message in the sentence has been "cognitively recoded" or interpreted correctly.

Don't try to correct this type of error. Let them continue to read as long as it makes sense. Remember substitutions and omissions are normal. Adult readers do this all the time.

Step 4

Recognize The Early Warning Signs

Many students get confused over what reading is. Many think reading is finishing the page. Many think reading is simply saying sounds aloud. These students make poor mistakes. These students need help.

A student who reads, "The map is tell," for the sentence: "The man is tall," is making a poor mistake. The sentence has no meaning. Students must be helped to recognize poor mistakes.

Sometimes students simply go too fast and are not aware of what they have just said. They need time to process what they heard.

Give them a chance to self-correct. Don't immediately correct them. Self-correcting is a very positive sign.

Step 5

Help Your Student Self-Correct

Follow this procedure if your student can't self-correct. First, bring the mistake to their attention. Read it aloud the way they said it. Ask them if what you just read makes sense. Ask them if it sounds right. Second, give them a choice. Repeat the sentence incorrectly. Then, say the sentence correctly. Ask them which one sounds better—which one makes sense. And ask them what they would do to correct it.

Always try to remind them that reading must make sense. The goal is to gain meaning—not to finish the page.

Let them know that you will help them as often as they need it.

Step 6

Become A Model

You are one of the most important persons in your student's life. You are a model. They never stop watching you. They watch how you act and they watch how you react. Words are not enough. It is what you do that counts.

Be sure to speak positively about books. You must demonstrate an infectious enthusiasm for reading. Talk to your student about books you read or had read to you. Talk about your favorite books. Talk about books that made you sad or happy or mad. Let your student know that you enjoyed the reading experience.

Step 7

The Five Finger Test

The Five Finger Test is very quick and simple way to measure the suitability of reading material. Have the student read a selected paragraph or two from the story you are about to read. Have the student put a finger down every time he/she makes a mistake. Stop using that material when the fifth finger hits the page.

Step 8

Demonstrate What Good Reading Sounds Like

Demonstrate what good reading sounds like. Let your students hear you read aloud. Show expression and inflection in your voice. Talk about how a question sounds and how it differs from a statement. Let them hear what should happen when a sentence ends in an exclamation mark.

Ask your students to listen carefully while you read a sentence two different ways. Ask them to be ready to tell you which way reading sounds the best. Make the first reading very slow and with no expression. For the second reading become a "ham." Play a role! Have fun! Read it this time with expression and enthusiasm!

Ask your student which reading sounded best. Ask them to read it exactly the way you did. Joke with them if they feel funny about doing this. Try to help them relax.

Step 9

Watch How You Criticize

Words are powerful. They can soothe and they can cause pain. Words are most powerful when they are uttered by someone important in your student's life such as a friend, a teacher, or a parent.

Words are not equal. Negative words are more powerful than positive words. One good word does not make up for one bad word. In fact, it might take as many as 100 good words to cancel out the impact of one bad word. So be careful when giving criticism. Hold your tongue. Above all else, avoid words and phrases such as, "Is that the best you can do?" "I'm ashamed of you!" and "What a dummy!"

Avoid sarcasm. Your students probably can't deal with it. And what's worse, your students might believe you mean what you say.

Step 10

Check Out What Your Body Is Saying

Be aware of your nonverbal communication. Verbal and nonverbal messages must match. They must be in harmony. Disharmony exists when your words are saying "yes" and your body is saying "no." Disharmony causes garbled messages. Your students can become confused and might not act in an appropriate way.

Nonverbal signs of approval include such things as: maintaining eye contact, leaning toward them, smiles, winks, nods and pats on the back. Try to use them often.

Step 11

Don't Be Misled By Grade Level

All beginning reading material is not equal. Some third grade stories are easier to understand and read than some first grade material. Some paragraphs and sentences are easier to read than others—even though they are in the same story! So don't assume that the story is one that your students can read simply on the basis of grade level.

The quickest and most accurate way to assess whether a story is appropriate for your students is by demonstration. Have your students read the story aloud. If they can read the story with little or no difficulty, the story is appropriate. If they can't read it by themselves, don't immediately assume they are to blame.

First check the story for appropriateness. Story appropriateness is based on three factors: content, style, and grammar.

Step 12

Check The Story Content

There are going to be some stories your student will find hard to read because your student does not have the necessary background and experiences to relate to the story. When this happens, reading comprehension will be affected.

Ask yourself if the story is about something your student has done, seen, or heard about. If you're not sure, ask your student to tell you something about the subject matter or read a sentence and ask him/her to explain what he/she thinks it means.

When your student shows confusion, stop reading and start explaining. Talk about what the story is about. Discuss relevant terms. Explain why characters are named the way they are. Be sure your student understands. Don't just take his/her word for it.

Step 13

Watch Your Student's Eyes

Many students will say they understand even when they don't. They don't want to look foolish. Watch your students' eyes. The eyes are a mirror of the mind. Look for understanding. If you don't see it, try again.

Try to explain it a different way. Try to relate it to something your student already knows. Don't push it; give it your best shot. If it is still difficult for your student to relate to, leave it. Close the book. Skip that particular story. Don't embarrass, don't scold, and don't get angry!

Step 14

Check the Story's Style

There are going to be some stories that your students will not relate to due to the author's writing style. This is especially true when it comes to the heavy use of names and personal pronouns.

Stories that are about familiar names and places and activities will always be easiest to read. The more the story moves away from common ideas, names, and places in your students' immediate world, the more difficult it will be for your students to read.

Listen to your student read or attempt to read. Are they having difficulty with the people's names or the names of places or are there strange words or phrases used in the story? If the answer is yes, the problem is within the material, and not within your students. The easiest solution is to tell them the names. Don't waste time asking them to "sound out" strange names they will probably never see again.

Step 15

Check the Story's Grammar

Grammar plays an important role in determining how well a student will read. Some stories are written using sentences that are easier to read.

The easiest sentence to read is a simple sentence. A simple sentence is a sentence that has only one subject, one verb and one object ("The man likes dogs."). Simple sentences do not contain embedded clauses and phrases ("The man, who lives on my street, likes dogs."). Simple sentences do not have a heavy use of adjectives, adverbs, and phrases. Simple sentences are short in length (no more than 8 to 10 words). Simple sentences are complete sentences.

Stories written in simple active declarative sentences are the easiest to read. Sentences that are long and complex will cause breakdowns. Be careful when you ask a student to read these sentences. Read these sentences aloud. Break the sentence down into more understandable parts.

Step 16

Help Your Student Become A Better Listener

Students who listen well will become better readers. Listening is a key to the development of reading comprehension. It is the key in the development of a student's meaningful vocabulary. Students with a strong meaningful vocabulary have more words that they can relate to in print.

Listening skills can be developed. You can help develop these skills. Students who are preoccupied with other things cannot attend to a task. Students need to see value in the listening activity. Discuss the value of the information and try to relate it to something they already know and/or respect.

Students, of any age, learn best when they are actively involved in the listening task. Talk to them and not at them. Try to have them participate with you. Carry on a discussion with them. Praise them for their participation.

Step 17

Help Your Student Listen For Directions

Students need to learn how to listen to directions. It is essential for academic success. For younger students, start with one basic command ("draw a person on this page"). Watch how they do. Ask yourself if it was too easy or too hard. Change it if it was too hard. Increase the complexity of the task if it was too easy ("draw a person with a black hat and a brown dog").

Move on to two and then three and then four direction commands. Have them act out commands. Use manipulative objects. Make it a game. Have fun. Enjoy.

Step 18

Help Your Student Recall Information

Tell your students that you are going to play a listening game. Let them know the purpose of the activity ("I want to see how well you can listen and remember what was read."). Read them a story. Make sure they listen to you read the story. Ask them questions from the story you just read.

Ask the questions in the order the information appears in the story. If they can't remember, go back to that part of the story. Read it again. Remind them to listen carefully for the answer as you read the part again. Use more sophisticated and complex material for older students. Don't let age prevent them from improvement.

Step 19

Learn the Difference Between Factual Questions and Inferential Questions

Factual questions are closed questions—they limit the number of responses a student can make. "What is the name of the boy in the story?" Is an example of a closed question. There is only one answer—the boy's name. No other answer will be correct.

Inferential questions (or open-ended questions) are not limited. The responses can vary as long as they make sense. "What do you think is a good name for the boy in the story?" Is an example of an open-ended question.

Vary your use of factual and inferential questions. Listen to their responses. Do they do better with one type of question? Do they need help with another type of question?

Step 20

Help Expand Your Students' Vocabulary

Take the opportunity to develop your students' language. Language is essential to good reading. Students with a good command of language will become better readers. Students with a limited command of the language will have difficulty reading. Case closed; improve their language!!!

Turn the reading into a language lesson. Have your student listen for new words. Have them try to guess their meaning on the basis of how they are used in the story. Discuss the new words.

Don't become upset if they cannot restate a word's meaning. Students need time to digest a word before they can use it themselves. Relax. Hearing words being used in a meaningful context is the first step in this process. Receptive language (what they understand) always comes before expressive language (what they can state). So don't judge them on what they say.

Step 21

Help Your Student Listen To Different Kinds of Reading Material

Let your students hear plays, poems, rhymes, short stories and other forms of literature. Don't worry if they can't comprehend everything that is being read to them. Your purpose is to prepare them for future contact. You are helping them "tune in" to the unique characteristics of different types of literature.

The more contact the better, as long as you are the one doing the reading. Don't expect them to read this material independently.

Step 22

Help Your Students Listen To Discussions

Have them listen to discussions. Let them participate in discussions. Set the proper example. Talk and listen to your student. Set aside a time when you can talk to your students without interruptions.

Reserve a quiet place and some time where you and your students can talk. Let them know you are interested in what they have to say, and then really listen.

Step 23

Establish A Daily Reading Time

According to *What Works, Research About Teaching And Learning,* published by the U.S. Department of Education (1986), "Students improve their reading by reading a lot. Reading achievement is directly related to the amount of reading students do in school and home."

Reading is like any other ability, the more students practice, the better they get. Students need to practice reading. They need to learn the process. They need to learn what reading is. Unfortunately, what they need and what they get are two different things.

Set aside reading time in the classroom or, for our parents, at home. And just as importantly, don't waste it. Make the maximum use of this time. Learn how to manage this time effectively. To make the most out of your home reading time:

1. Have all the reading materials ready at the start of the reading time, 2. Get the reading started quickly, 3. Get your student involved immediately, and 4. Keep your student involved throughout the entire reading time.

Step 24

Broaden Your Students' Experiences

Students learn by doing. Talking about something is good. Seeing something is better. Actually doing it is best. Whenever possible, try expanding your students' firsthand experiences.

Take your students on field trips such as the zoo, or the park. Don't let a lack of money stop you. Look for places within your neighborhood that you can go. Contact your church or local civic groups. Take nothing for granted. No experience is too small or insignificant. Look for opportunities in normal everyday occurrences such as in the grocery store, or the bank, or the cleaners, or the drug store. Can't leave the building? No problem. Bring the neighborhood to you. Bring in speakers representing all of the above.

Take the initiative. Don't wait for them to ask you questions. Do it first. Never assume they will always ask. Never assume they will always know. If they do already know—so what? What's the harm?

Step 25

Read to Your Students

Reading aloud to your students is one of the best ways to help your students become better readers. Reading aloud provides an opportunity to experience the total reading process. Reading aloud is better than using workbooks or other formal teaching tools.

Research has shown that reading to your students especially after they are in the third grade or higher will actually improve their reading as much as having them read by themselves.

Plan for discussion. The discussion about the story is as important as the story itself. Use this as an opportunity to expand your students' knowledge and insight of language.

Use a variety of different questions. Don't limit yourself. Try to blend the use of both open-ended and closed questions. In other words, mix some "why do you think" questions with the "who, what, where and when" types.

Remember to show enthusiasm when you read. Be animated. Have fun. Make it enjoyable.

Step 26

Read It Again

Students are not turned off by repetition. They need it. They rely on it. They crave it. If you don't believe this, then ask yourself: how many times does a student ask the same question? Or want to hear the same story read aloud? Or watch the same TV show? Or listen to the same song on the radio?

Repetition does not bore students during the initial stages of a learning task. It is a must. Your student must have it in order to practice.

Repetition provides them with the necessary amount of exposures they need to master the skill. It makes them comfortable with the material. It eliminates the guesswork. They will know what to expect. They will know what is coming next.

Step 27

Show Your Students How to Use Story Clues to Identify Unfamiliar Words

Show your students how the story can help to identify unfamiliar words. Imagine you are reading a story about rooms in a house and your student can't identify the word "kitchen." What could you do to help him/her figure the word out? 1) You can restate the story's theme—what the story is all about. ("Do you remember the story about the names of rooms in a house? What are the names of some of the rooms in a house called?") 2) Ask him/her to try to skip that word and finish the whole sentence. ("Can you read the rest of the words in the sentence: I think the "_____" is the best room in the house.") 3) Have your student choose a word that would make sense in the sentence. Reread the sentence before it and the sentence after it to see if the choice makes sense. ("Let's see if bathroom makes the most sense. Listen while I read and tell me if bathroom makes the most sense. 'The next room has water and sinks in it. I think the bathroom is the best room in the house. I like to go there when I want to get something to eat.' ")

Allow him/her to change his/her guess if it does not fit. ("Do you still think 'bathroom' is the best choice?") Praise him/her for a good choice and the ability to find the best possible answer.

Step 28

Show Your Student How to Use Story Clues to Unlock the Meaning of Unknown Words

Show your student how the story can help unlock the meaning of unknown words. Ask your student to listen to how the word is used in the story. Ask your student to let the other words in the story help him/her discover what the unknown word means.

Be as verbal as possible. Explain why one choice might be better than another. Make him/her aware of the clues that an author gives to help clarify words. Tell how good readers do this type of guessing every time they read. Point out the difference between a good guess (one that makes sense) and a poor one (one that does not make sense).

Step 29

Show How to Use Story Clues to Deal With Multiple-Meaning Words

Show your student how a story can help him/her decide the correct meaning in a multiple-meaning word. Talk about multiple-meaning words. Talk about how words can have more than one meaning. Give him/her examples ("What does the word 'run' mean?" "That's right, the word 'run' can mean many different things: such as having to run down the street, or a home run in a baseball game, or a run in a woman's stocking.").

Tell them that what a word means is based on how the word is used in the story. Explain to them that the words and sentences around the word give a clue to its meaning. Turn this into a language lesson.

Step 30

Show How to Use Story Clues to Deal With Multiple-Sounding Words

Let your students know about words that look the same but are said differently. Give them examples of homonyms. ("Today, I will read the same story we read yesterday," or "The girl with the blue bow in her hair took a bow.") Help them understand that how to pronounce a multiple-sounding word is based on how the word is used in the story.

Don't be upset if they have trouble understanding all of this. The main thing is to have them become aware of just how confusing our language is. Our goal, at this time, is awareness and not understanding. Awareness is the first step in the understanding process.

> *Teaching someone how to read is a gift. You are helping your student unlock his or her's self-esteem and success. Remember to be patient, and to always stay positive. Be sure to follow these tips to ensure success for you and your students!*

Appendix C:

Failure Free Reading Testimonials

Failure Free Reading and the CCC (The Center City Consortium)

Failure Free Reading helps to fulfill the CCC's Goal to "create centers of educational excellence that give witness to the fact that, given the right learning atmosphere and a culture of high expectation, all students can and will reach their highest potential."

Teachers, parents, administrators, and students all play a key role when it comes to setting goals and establishing a game plan (objectives) for each child. Flexibility that accommodates the diversity of learning styles, interests, and backgrounds of our students is paramount in the classroom. When we are ready to accept that instructional goals don't have to be the same for each learner, as traditional ISD models would suggest, we are on the brink of success.

As teachers, we all must recognize that learning is always constantly evolving by nature. Everyone learns at his or her own speed and latches on to those concepts/components that personally peak their interest or, that they deem necessary for their own survival/success. It's human nature.

The **Failure Free Reading Program** meets students where they are, assessing their ability level at the very beginning. The students are then guided through each lesson at a pace that is comfortable to them. Repetition is key. The program introduces a series of five word lessons in different formats that allow the student to see how the word is used in multiple settings.

Children master skills and content in stages so there need to be incremental benchmarks that reward and encourage students at every stage. This may seem like an overwhelming mandate, until we factor in technology. State of the art technologically assisted programs such as **Failure Free Reading** can accommodate and monitor several different learning styles and learning goals at once.

The Center City Consortium is always seeking ways to enrich the learning environments in their schools. Teachers are encouraged to credit the learner's existing knowledge and use that data/experiential bank to help connect new information. This is another area where **Failure Free Reading** can prove to be an invaluable asset.

Even in schools where the content is set, an integrated student-centered approach that allows the students to hone into certain areas and skim through or pass over others could be employed. All this is a scary concept for many educators who are still anxious about trying any method that differs from any pedagogical techniques they were taught and with which they have become comfortable.

Students can be taught and trained to remember certain information or complete certain tasks. We must be mindful however of whether we are affording them enough time to process, make sense of, and /or use new words or concepts while we are herding them through textbooks and work-sheets, trying to finish the curriculum in the school year—as if just getting to page 506 of their Reading Textbooks prove that real learning has tran-spired in our classrooms.

This is where many reading programs fall short. Slower readers may fall behind because the vocabulary in their textbooks/literature sets may be too difficult to grasp. Fluency that promotes comprehension in this case would be sacrificed. These students will have difficulty answering posed comprehension questions. Although their test scores will ultimately reveal in gaps in their understanding, there usually isn't enough time in the sched-ule to revisit passages or vocabulary with which they had difficulty. **Failure Free Reading** does not move ahead until the learner has mastered the les-son that they are on. The teacher can immediately assess whether each stu-dent's progress is aligned with his or her individual goals and /or the class' standards. If the student's scores show that the desired level of mastery has not been achieved, the teacher can change the student's Bookmark from their workstation and have him/her repeat the lesson. Likewise, students that aren't being challenged by their grade level reading material can have their Bookmark advanced.

There are three elements that Failure Free Reading employs to help set up objectives and goals in the classroom.

> **The Bridge**—In this phase, the computer initiates a series of initia-tion activities to determine what the student already knows.
>
> **Lesson/ Evaluation**—Lessons and periodic assessments at every phase are meant to keep student progressing through multiple lev-els of understanding.
>
> **Exhibit**—Students demonstrate their understanding of the material by taking a Post-lesson Exam. Each student also receives work-book that based on the Reading Level they have been assigned. The workbook activities help reinforce and apply what the student had learned.

What are Teachers, Administrators, and Students saying about Failure Free Reading?

"I would love to begin implementing the Failure Free reading Program at Immaculate. It's like Waterford for older kids. Students in all my grade levels can benefit from the individualized instruction."

—*Ms. Gillian Pratt*, Principal, Immaculate Conception School

"I have worked with Failure Free Reading for 2 years and have seen my students demonstrate remarkable progress. Students even enjoy using words that they learn in the program. Many of my students have become better test takers in general as they are quite accustomed to logging on and independently sitting for a 45-minute block and the computer tutors them through various levels. I monitor the I-KNOW online exams as well and I have seen that the students enrolled in the program are usually less anxious and fidgety during the test sessions. Their reading scores have also improved on the State Exams since enrolling in the program.

I have had students say that they like the program because…

"It's like you can just do your own thing. You don't have to worry about what everybody else is doing."

"It helps me with my reading because now I know what a lot of the words mean."

"I like working with the computer. It is fun and I like to see how I'm doing at the Teacher's station. That way I know if I really understand things the way I think I do."

"It teaches me big words that I never knew before and my family doesn't even know. I feel smart."

—*Ms. Akema Sarr*, Technology Teacher, St. Francis de Sales & Immaculate Conception School

"Failure Free Reading sounds like an excellent program to use in the fourth grade. We are currently using the Open Court Program. As teachers, we are responsible for making sure our students become and remain good readers, writers, and spellers. Therefore, my reason for wanting this program for my students is simple. The program will enhance their skills as well as their computer skills. It appears that the program will help students with proofreading, developing visual memory, and apply spelling words in reading."

—*Ms. Telita Estes*, Fourth Grade Teacher, Immaculate Conception School

"From all that I have heard about Failure Free Reading, I can't figure out why this isn't in more of our schools. I need something like this for my class immediately. I have so many children on so many different levels this year that is truly is a struggle to make sure that everyone's needs are being met. Our Open Court Reading Program works well if you are truly on the third grade level, but I have a few students who are above and below the standards provided by this system. Failure Free Reading can help some of my struggling students learn the vocabulary and spelling they need to benefit from standard grade level material. I even see the program acting as an enrichment tool for some of my advanced students. We can't go wrong with such an individually tailored program. I will begin using it the week that it's approved."

—Ms. Zanette Gunn, Third Grade Teacher, Immaculate Conception School

Submitted by:

Ms. Akema Sarr, Technology Teacher, St. Francis de Sales & Immaculate Conception School

Baldwin County School System

Milledgeville, Georgia 31061

Dr. Joe Lockavitch
Failure Free Reading

Dear Dr. Lockavitch:

We piloted the *Joseph's Readers* program in our 5 week Title 1 summer School this summer. At the initial training, several teachers, whom I know have a track record of success in teaching children to read, were not too positive toward the program. Many felt it was too repetitious, too boring, and would likely turn kids off to reading. This made me very uneasy since we have invested a rather large sum for software and materials. However, when I rechecked with these same teachers at the end of the 5 weeks, they all said they still thought it repetitive and boring; however, to a soul, they agreed children loved it,…especially those children who had seldom if every experienced success with reading. One of the summer school teachers was contacted by a parent who said her summer school child came home saying, "Ma, I don't want summer school to be over. I just love them books we been a 'reading'." When we can get a 9, 10 or 11-year child to wish summer school not to end, we must be doing something terribly wrong or something terribly right. I prefer to think the latter.

Ms. Giese is providing our Title 1 teachers some in-service on *Joseph's Readers* today. She is doing a fantastic job, and she promises to check back with these same teachers during the school year to see how the program is progressing. I anticipate we will have similar results with your program during the regular school years as we had in summer school. I certainly hope this turns out to be true.

Sincerely,
Robert Lamb
Robert Lamb, Ed.D.

Greenville County Schools

Where Enlightening Strikes
Monica Wills
Project Specialist
Federal Programs

Failure Free Reading

Dear Failure Free Reading:

It is my pleasure to provide a letter of recommendation to comply with section J of the South Carolina Department of Education's 2005-2006 application to be an approved Supplemental Service Provider.

Failure Free Reading has been an approved provider of Supplemental Educational Services for Greenville County Schools for the 2004-05 school years. Failure Free Reading has been regarded as one of the most congenial providers of Supplemental Educational Services for Greenville County. The integrity and quality of their services is phenomenal. They have modeled exemplary professionalism and have performed admirably with high regards. In working with Greenville County Schools, they have been considerate, helpful, and have cooperatively provided anything requested. Both parents and students alike have been pleased with services rendered. Students thoroughly enjoy attending sessions and believe that they are benefiting educationally from Failure Free Reading's curriculum.

Greenville County Schools endorses their application to continue providing services for students eligible to receive SES for the 2005-06 school years.

Sincerely,
Monica A. Wills

Failure Free Reading

July 12, 2005

I would like to express my gratitude for being given the opportunity to work with Failure Free Reading, both personally and professionally.

Failure Free is a program that ensures the proficient, competent reading ability of all grade school children. The program works with low income, multicultural communities, possessing bright articulate students who are eager to reap the benefits of this curriculum.

Living in New York City, many of our children are at risk. Level I is English Language Learners and special needs. Although there are many issues challenging the effectiveness and over all success of our children, **"Failure Free"** understands the need for every child to succeed, feel proud, grow morally and have a sound social education.

Middle school children are some of the hardest to reach. Years of being low achievers, they now feel there is no hope, I'm dumb, stupid, I can't learn, and so they simply give up. **Failure Free** changes all of that, allowing students to work independently at their level with computers. This ensures privacy and builds well-needed self-esteem, which is crucial for middle school children.

To see a smile on the face of a student, who was once timid, or demure to embrace their opened arms, is a true testimonial.

Additionally, it is important to note **Failure Free Reading** has displayed a professional versatile demeanor, in a diverse body of circumstances, effectively contributing to the expedient resolve of parental understanding and participation.

Again thank you **Failure Free**, for being focused on the paramount objective…the future of our children.

Sincerely,
Patricia Williams

Lafourche Parish School Board

Office of Superintendent
Thibodaux, Louisiana

January 26, 2004

Dr, Joseph Lockavitch

Dear Dr. Lockavitch:

Lafourche Parish has used Failure Free Reading with non-readers for the last 5 years. Failure Free Reading has been excellent for this population of students. A number of students have been able to participate in regular classroom activities and have dramatically increased their reading abilities. We have used Failure Free Reading throughout the District.

Sincerely,
Linda Dangerfield, Supervisor
Special Education Department

CECIL COUNTY PUBLIC SCHOOLS

Division of Education Services
Elkton, MD

December 8, 2003

To Whom It May Concern:

As the Instructional Coordinator for English Language Arts, I approved the implementation of the Failure Free Reading program at Elkton Middle School, Cherry Hill Middle School, and North East Middle School for the 2003 summer school session. Some of the students chosen for the implementation have received special education services and have a history of low reading scores. In addition, the motivation of these students to engage in reading is very low.

Failure Free Reading provided teachers and students three components for success: teaching strategies and materials, technology, and consistent text materials. The technology, specifically its proprietary talking software, was loaded onto our existing computers. Teachers were provided initial professional development and consistent, regular contact during the implementation period from the Failure Free Reading staff.

During the short summer school period, many students were able to, for the first time, read age and grade level appropriate materials. Many of them were able to complete the grade level materials and move onto some higher level vocabulary and more involved, higher order thinking skill reading material. Our teachers were very pleased with the results of the Failure Free Reading implementation. Based on their input, Cecil County has ordered or plans to order additional materials from Failure Free Reading to further the implementation into the other middle schools and some high schools.

Martin Haberl
Instructional Coordinator for English Language Arts

December 17, 2003
Louisiana Department of Education
Baton Rouge, Louisiana

Dear Department:

I am pleased to submit this letter of support for the application of Failure Free Reading to the State Department of Education to become a provider of supplemental services to underachieving schools in Louisiana.

As I understand the design and intent of the supplemental services initiative, I believe Failure Free is the logical choice of programs to help children and youth learn to read at grade level and to help grade-level readers dramatically improve their vocabulary skills.

When I became aware of the Failure Free Reading program in 1995, I helped initiate a pilot test program in a 7th grade class at the Louisiana School for the deaf. Deaf students internationally have profoundly low average reading achievement and the students at the program using Failure Free methods and materials showed remarkable and exciting results—a promising breakthrough in the teaching of reading to students who are deaf. Subsequently, I helped promote the Failure Free program to elementary, middle and high schools throughout Louisiana during 1997-98.

Before I left the state in 1999 to become Academic Dean of the Alexandria (Virginia) campus of Strayer University, I had helped train hundreds of teachers, administrators and parents throughout Louisiana and even parents and reading tutors. The Failure Free program exists in some part of about half of the school districts in the state and in a high number of the Catholic Schools in Baton Rouge and New Orleans. There is a strong "Failure Free presence" in Louisiana.

I know first hand that the program does what it claims it can do—train non-readers or poor readers (two or more grades below grade-level) to read at grade level, usually in one semester. This includes early grades, middle grades, junior high and high school, as well as special education students— Down Syndrome, Learning Disabled, mildly retarded, and ADHD!

Failure Free is easy for teachers to manage and it fits well within almost any classroom configuration or program schedule. It can be ideal as an after-school or before school or at-home intervention. It works. Whether it is for one or two students, a small group or large group, it works!

I can think of no faster way to improve the report card of low performing schools than to provide access of low performing students to the Failure Free program. I recommend Failure Free Reading without hesitation.

Sincerely,
William V. Schipper, Ph.D
Academic Dean, Alexandria Campus
Strayer University

Dear Failure Free Reading,

I am so proud and overjoyed with my daughter's progress with the Failure Free Reading. Her confidence and self-esteem have improved dramatically, as has her reading fluency and comprehension. There was a visible improvement after every session and after only eight sessions her school grade improved to the point she was reading on grade level. When report cards came out she was on the "A" honor roll for the very first time, having improved in every subject.

    The teachers and staff are just wonderful. I am amazed at the involvement of everyone associated with the program from the receptionist to the President and Founder. There is always an encouraging work and time to listen to a story being read by a proud student. I am so happy that I found and enrolled my daughter in the Failure Free Reading program. Thank You!!

Pam Rimer
(Daughter—Courtney Rimer)

Scottsdale YISA Cadets

El Paso, Texas

Dr. Lockavitch,

I would like to share with you the success my students are accomplishing with the Failure Free Reading here at Scotsdale Elementary. I am the E.S.L. teacher and I am using the Teal level reading program that is designed to target students in grade 4 through 6. This year, however, I adapted the program to 3rd graders and the results have been pleasantly astonishing. I service 30 English as Second Language students in all. They come in groups of five (from grades 3 to 6). This is my second year using the program and I am very pleased with the results my students are achieving. I personally appreciate the program for the following reasons.

- The lessons and material are teacher friendly.
- The reading lessons, the worksheets and the computer program compliment and reinforce each other.
- The spelling program on the computer software is also very helpful in helping the students with pronunciation and the spelling of the words.
- The materials and lessons are challenging, age-appropriate, and the program allows the students to work on a pace that is suitable for them to learn successfully.
- There is immediate successful progress in reading and understanding of lessons.
- The Vocabulary flash cards also have been a great help. I made a copy for each of my students to review and practice at home. We also play a vocabulary spelling game in the classroom. The students must read, translate meaning into Spanish, use it in a complete sentence, and spell the word correctly in order to keep the vocabulary card. Of course the student with the most cards wins.
- I have received positive feedback from the students' homeroom teacher.

My principal, Mrs. Olivas, evaluated me this year and she was so impressed with the lesson and the progress the students have achieved that purchased your Orange Failure Free Reading Level, in which I will be using next year with 2nd grade. The US Department of Education nominated our school and four others across the nation with the National Title I Distinguished Schools Recognition Program Award, not only because of our academic achievement, but also because of our school's selection by the Texas Education Agency as one of the 12 Reading Spotlight Schools. I strongly feel that your reading program as well as the many others that we have adopted and implemented in our school has most certainly helped us reach these great honors.

Sincerely,
Norma Herrera
E.S.L. Teacher

July 6, 2005

Ladies and Gentlemen:

Let me take this opportunity to tell you that I had the good fortune to have worked as a Failure Free Reading tutor during the academic school year 2004-2005 at Roberto Clemente CIS 166X. I believe that I echo my colleagues' sentiments when expressing the wonderful experience that we had helping our students with the Failure Free Reading program.

First of all, as tutors we received the computer and literacy training that enabled us to adequately help our students. At the same time, we received the assistance and support of Ms. Patricia Williams and Stephen Yelity when requested.

Secondly, it must be indicated that Failure Free Reading was helpful to our students, as it addressed the fundamental academic deficiencies of the population that is served at our school (English Language Learners and Academic Performance Level I students). The academic progress was evident as the students learned and incorporated new words to their vocabularies. Furthermore, in conversations with several teachers, they articulated the academic improvement displayed by their students as the Failure Free Reading program progressed.

Another component indicative of the Failure Free Reading success at Roberto Clemente CIS 166X is the enthusiasm exhibited by the students as they noticed their academic progress. This enthusiasm was also expressed by the parents in their desire to participate in the program.

Finally, we, at Roberto Clemente CIS 166X feel that the Failure Free Reading program was a success at our school, and should be incorporated into our curricula for the coming academic school year, as the students demonstrated academic progress that was recognized and appreciated by teachers and parents alike.

Sincerely,
Ezequiel S. Zulueta

Bienville High School

Bienville, Louisiana

July 10, 1998

Dear Failure Free Reading:

The Failure Reading Program at the Bienville high School was a success for the school year 1997-98. The children really looked forward to coming to the center to work with this program.

Bienville is a small school with a population of 197. Most students receive free or reduced lunches.

Eight students were chosen from the first to third grade. The first grade were students having trouble in reading. The second and third grade students were chosen by the lowest CAT scores.

I, Clara Powell, was impressed with the program. I saw third grade students who could not read a complete sentence, now, reading whole stories without missing the first word. All my students were eager to read and their self-esteem grew by leaps and bounds. Even the first grade students became comfortable in placing words in ABC order.... I believe that this program will work for students having trouble with reading. I enjoy teaching students who look forward to coming to class.

Sincerely,
Clara Powell
Failure Free Reading Teacher

Bibliography

American Library Association. (2004). *National Center for Education Statistics (NCES)*.

Beck, I. L., Kucan, L., McKeown, M. G. (2002*). Bringing Words to Life: Robust Vocabulary Instruction*. New York, New York: The Guilford Press.

Bennett, William J. (1986). *What Works: Research About Teaching and Learning*. U.S. Department of Education.

Biancarosa, G., Snow, C. E. (2004). *Reading next-A Vision for action and research in middle and high school literacy: A report to Carnegie Corporation of New York*. Washington, DC: Alliance for Excellent Education.

Biemiller, Andrew. (1999). *Language and Reading Success*. Newton Upper Falls, Massachusetts: Brookline Books.

Burns, S.B., Griffin, P., Snow, C.E. (1998). *Preventing Reading difficulties in Young Children* (National research Council) National Academy Press, Washington, DC.

Coltheart, M., Jackson, N. E. (2001). *Routes to Reading Success and Failure*. New York, New York: Taylor and Francis.

Di Vesta, Francis J. (1974). *Language, Learning, and Cognitive Processes*. Monterey, California: Brooks/Cole Publishing Company.

Durkin, D. (1978-79). *What classroom observations reveal about reading comprehension instruction*. Reading Research Quarterly.

Green, Pollack, & Scarffe. (1995). *When Goldilocks went to the House of the Bears*. Mondo Publishing, Greenvale, NY.

Fuchs, D., Otaiba, S. A. (2002). *Characteristics of children who are unresponsive to early literacy intervention: A review of literature Remedial & Special Education*.

Harber, J. R. (1979). *Syntactic complexity: a necessary Ingredient in predicting readability. Journal of Learning Disabilities, 12,* 13-19.

Hargis, Charles H. (1982). *Teaching reading to handicapped children.* Love Publishing Company.

Hargis, C.H., Terhaar-Yonkers, M., Williams, P.C., Reed, M.T. (1992). *Tennessee Educator, 22*, 31-34.

Hargis, C.H. (2000). *Does the Case for Balanced Teaching Miss the Point? Contemporary Psychology.* APA Review of Books, 45(5), 522-525.

Hiebert, E. H. (1998). *Text matters in learning to read. Ann Arbor, Mich: Center for the Improvement of Early Reading Achievement.* University of Michigan.

Jimerson, Shane R. (2001). *Meta-Analysis of Grade Retention Research: Implications for Practice in the 21st Century.* School Psychology Review, 30(3), 420-437.

Johnson, D. J., Myklebust, H.R. (1967). *Learning Disabilities: Educational Principles and Practices.* New York, New York: Grune & Stratton, Inc.

Juel, C., Robert-Schneider, D. (1985). *The influence of basal readers on first grade reading.* Reading Research Quarterly, 20, 134–152.

Kuhn, M. R., Stahl, S.A. (2000). *Teaching Children to Learn Word Meanings From Context: A Synthesis and Some Questions. Journal of Literacy Research.*

McCormick, J. (1994). *A nonreader becomes a reader: a case of literacy acquisition by a severely disabled reader. Reading Research Quarterly,* April/May/June 1994, 157-176.

Menyuk, Paula (1999). *Reading and Linguistic Development.* Cambridge, Massachusetts: Brookline Books.

Rathvon, Natalie (1999). *Effective School Interventions: Strategies for Enhancing Academic Achievement and Social Competence.* New York, New York: The Guilford Press.

Richek, M.A., Stahl, S. A., and Vandevier, R. J. (1991). *Learning meaning vocabulary through listening: A sixth-grade replication.* National Reading Conference Yearbook, 40, 185-192.

Samuels, S.J. (1988). *Decoding and automaticity: Helping poor readers become automatic at word recognition. The Reading Teacher,* 41, 756-760.

Semel, Eleanor M., Wiig, Elisabeth H. (1980). *Language Assessment and intervention for the Learning Disabled.* Columbus, Ohio: Charles E. Merrill Publishing Company.

Seuss, Dr. (1960). *Green Eggs and Ham.* Random House Books for Young Readers.

Smith, Frank. (1979). *Reading Without Nonsense.* New York: Teachers College Press.

Smith. (1941). *Genetic Psychological Monographs.*

Stahl, Steven A. (1999). *Vocabulary Development.* Brookline, Massachusetts: Brookline Books.

Stanovich, K.E. (1980). *Toward an interactive-compensatory model of individual differences I the development of reading fluency.* Reading Research Quarterly, 16, 32-65.

Stanovich, K. E. (1986). *Matthew Effects in Reading: Some Consequences of Individual Differences in the Acquisition of Literacy.* Reading Research Quarterly.

Torgeson, J. (1997). *Preventing Reading Difficulties in Young Children.*

U.S. Department of Education. (1999). *Start Early, Finish Strong: How to Help Every Child Become a Reader.* America Reads Challenge.

About The Author

Dr. Joseph F. Lockavitch, a former classroom teacher, school psychologist, university professor, special education director, and applied researcher, is the author and developer of: The Failure Free Reading Program, *Don't Close the Book on Your Not-Yet Readers*, Joseph's Readers Talking Software for Non-Readers, Verbal Master-An Accelerated Vocabulary Program, and The Test of Lateral Awareness and Directionality.

Dr. Lockavitch is also the author of numerous published research articles. His most recent work can be found in the *Australian Journal of Learning Disabilities*, the *Journal of Learning Disabilities*, *Special Services in the Schools*, *The Journal of At-Risk Issues*, and *The Florida Reading Quarterly*.

A noted speaker who is listed in *Outstanding Teachers in Exceptional Education*, *Who's Who in American Education*, and *Who's Who in the South and Southwest*, Dr. Lockavitch has spent the past thirty years training thousands of teachers, parents and administrators across the nation on how to meet the unique needs of America's non-readers.

Featured on the PBS NewsHour with Jim Lehrer and mentioned on national radio shows such as: Tom Joyner, Dr. Laura, Mike Gallagher, and Michael Medved, Dr. Lockavitch holds a Doctorate of Education from Boston University and a Master of Science in Special Education from Southern Connecticut State University in New Haven, Connecticut.

He is currently the President of Failure Free Reading- an educational publishing and software development firm housed outside of Charlotte, North Carolina. Failure Free Reading has been used by thousands of teachers to serve hundreds of thousands of students in schools across the nation.

In addition, Failure Free Reading is one of the nation's most approved Supplemental Educational Service providers - directly serving over ten thousand students and clocking close to three hundred thousand tutoring hours.

Printed in the United States
109863LV00004BC/34-81/P

9 781598 583052